DISASTER SURVIVAL

Lieutenant Colonel Dennis V. Eclarin

Also by Lieutenant Colonel Dennis V Eclarin

Philippine Jungle Survival
Scout Ranger War Stories
Philippine Rebel Stories
Scout Ranger Combat Leadership
Scout Ranger Combat Guide
Scout Ranger Registry
Philippine Scout Rangers

ISBN   978 165 681 6849

Contact the author at
email: dennis_eclarin@yahoo.com
mobile: +63 917 819 8867

INTRODUCTION

For some strange reason, I started writing this book during the height of a typhoon. I first wrote:

"It is July 16, 2014. As I write, typhoon Glenda lashes out at Bicol, Quezon and Metro Manila. The gusty winds are howling outside our Metro Manila home. I can hear the branches of the huge mango tree beside our house crack. The two old coconut trees nearby may not withstand Glenda's stong winds.

At this time, many parents like me may be silently praying that the winds would not get stronger and the rain does not continue to pour. There is always the danger of flooding and damage to property if the typhoon worsens. Yet, we are prepared to move out and evacuate to a safer place, just as we have done a few times in the past, to save ourselves and most importantly, our children.

Our children seem oblivious to the damage the calamity may cause. They are busy playing games on their gadgets, possibly assuming they could ride out the storm on the sofa."

But disasters can happen. They come when we least expect them to. As I was finishing the draft of the introduction for this book, the big mango tree and one of the coconut trees fell, narrowly missing our cars. But the roof of our home was severly damaged by both trees. Disaster has struck.

Our roof leaked and my children were afraid — now aware of the danger such strong winds could bring. We immediately evacuated, leaving the driver and an assistant to mind the house.

With no extra clothes and just the most valuable documents and cash, we headed out, all five of us, into the storm. As I drove along the main street lined with old acacia trees, I kept praying that no branch would fall on us inside our van. As my wife and daughters nervously tucked themselves in at the back seat, my 10 year old son and I prayed that no freak accident would befall to us.

We found a hotel full of refugees like ourselves. Luckily, there was one room left. As I continued writing in the safety of the hotel room, I realized that countless other families are facing the full wrath of the typhoon. I prayed that no life will unnecessarily be taken away by this natural force that visits regularly.

More of these catastrophes will come. There is simply no doubt about that. Yet, families will cope each time a life – threatening situation arises.

I am writing this book as a reminder to parents and children that anything could happen. They must therefore be prepared for those agonizing hours, minutes and seconds when they will have to survive together, to face a calamity.

The relevance of this book cannot be underestimated. This is useful to parents and children alike, all of whom are potential disaster victims. I have included disaster survivor and responder stories to remind us of the realities we all face during a catastrophe. I have likewise included practical and tested survival techniques which, when practiced, can save your life and that of your family. May you heed the lessons from this book when the next disaster comes.

My family is now a veteran of at least five typhoons and floods. With God's grace, we survived them all, though in some instances, we were almost victims.

The winds are still strong as I finish this introduction. This, too, will come to pass in a few more hours. But another one will come in the near future. I hope when it does, the book would serve its purpose.

Contents

01

PREPARING FOR A DISASTER

CONSTANT THREAT OF A DISASTER

Ours is one of the most vulnerable countries in the world to disasters. Based on the United Nation's 2012 World Risk Index, the Philippines is the third country most at risk to disasters. This threat of a disaster happening anywhere and anytime does not go away. Thus, people must constantly be on alert.

Several types of calamities ravage our country every year. Making up at least 50% of the annual disasters that strike the Philippines, typhoons and storms surpass all other calamities in number of victims in related flooding and landslides brought about by these tropical cyclones.

Volcanic eruptions and earthquakes are not as regular and frequent but these are equally devastating to the affected communities. Tsunamis, droughts, tornados and a few other natural calamities also affect the Philippines regularly.

Faced with the constant threat of disruption in their family life and community functioning, Filipino families must brace for any disaster that comes. It is only in being prepared that we may be able to save ourselves.

Every community in our country is in a constant threat of a disaster.

One cannot really over prepare for a disaster. This comes so unpredictably that even the best preparations may not be enough. When typhoon Glenda hit Metro Manila, my family of five were so comfortable. Seconds later, we heard the loud thud of crashing branches as the 50-year old mango tree fell on our roof. Had it not been for a solid fence between that tree and the house, we would have been crushed. Indeed, no amount of preparation would have adequately prepared us for what had happened.

Like most victims of catastrophes, we did not see any potential danger. Yet, like all survivors, my family had the presence of mind to pack and leave, without the hysterics, without panicking.

Your reaction to a disaster comes from your psychological preparation.

In my experience with handling crises and emergencies, every second counts. With God's grace, there may be a few minutes left to save yourself and other members of your family. It is how you instinctively react to danger that determines whether you live or die.

IT IS ALL IN THE MIND

This is what we call "presence of mind" in combat. In the chaos of rampaging bullets, a soldier must decide which action to take: to fire or maneuver. In a disaster situation, there is a similar imminent threat to your life. You must be in a state of mind to make the correct decision to bring your loved ones to safety. One wrong decision and you all perish. No matter how extreme the situation you face, you must still have the solid and logical frame of mind to conquer your fear and come out alive. Let me share with you the story of a fourteen year old young lady who survived the worst ordeal of her life.

A FLASH FLOOD SURVIVOR SPEAKS

Before the storm, my parents and kid sister, then only 2 years old, eagerly waited for Christmas. Though we were not well-off, our parents asked us what we wanted to do for Christmas and where we wanted to go. They both took a leave from their work that week just to bring us around.

When Friday came, only my kid sister and I were left at home. We played just like normal kids do, and after dinner, I put her to sleep. My parents came in after that, and then I went to sleep too.

"Wake up! wake up!" my mother said. It was 10 pm. My fourteen-year old sister and I are not used to being awakened in the middle of the night.

"There is flood water inside our house!" she exclaimed. I could not believe her because floods were rare in our part of the country. I looked out the window and there was a raging sea of muddy water from the mountains with all sorts of debris rushing out to sea. In the meantime, the water inside our house has reached the second floor. I was alarmed!

"Help us! Help us!" yelled my mom. But there was an eerie silence.

"Help! Help!" shouted my father. There were no replies. In

the meantime, the water level on our floor was steadily rising. My father had my young sister in his arms while my uncle who had two kids, aged 3 and one year old, had his in his arms, too. My mother was panicking as she packed our important belongings.

The water was rising fast. My father had the presence of mind to make a hole on the roof of our house. With all the love of a father who had a family in mortal danger, he led us out through that hole in the roof of our house.

But our freedom was short-lived. Slowly, the force of the flood waters rocked its weak foundation. As it tilted, my father told us to grab the tree beside our house. It was hard for me to grab the protruding tree branch all by myself. My uncle did a heroic act and grabbed me out of our house as it was flushed out into the sea. I was lucky but my two cousins were not. In the process of rescuing me, my uncle lost his two young kids. Both were instantly swept away by the fast flood waters. My uncle, having lost both kids, tried to swim towards them. I have not seen him or my cousins ever again.

Meanwhile, my family was in the fight of our lives. My father clung desperately onto a tree, with my two year old sister in his arms. My mother and I were in another tree as the flood waters raged and debris hit us. After an hour in that situation, in total darkness, and only the cries of my sister competing with the deadly rush of the water, the two trees slowly gave in to the strength of the raging flood. My father desperately tried to save us.

"Hold on tight," he told me and my mother.

"I love you *ate*," whispered my sister who, at two years old, could already talk. As she uttered those words, I saw my father, my mother and sister taken away by the deadly waters. I did not know what happened but I was also drowning and swept off by the river after that.

By the grace of God, a small log bumped into me. I grabbed it, and held on. I was on top of that log, looking at the dark sky, and prayed.

A FLASH FLOOD SURVIVOR SPEAKS

Caught by a flashflood, I floated with a log into the open sea until I was moored into an island eight hours after.

"Lord, save my family!" I murmured. I just kept on praying that I will still see my family. I could not see anything. All I knew was that I was on top of a log, floating on the deep blue sea.

Tired from the struggle, I slept on that log and later, I felt something grainy on my skin. It was beach sand!

"It's a miracle!" I thought to myself. As the sun rose, I found myself among many other survivors on that island. The water current must have brought us all there. Thus, there were many people crying, all searching for their loved ones. I saw mothers waiting, looking for their children. For some reason, I did not cry at that moment. I just wanted for a sign that my family was alive.

Rescue workers gathered us in an evacuation center. I prayed hard that my parents and sisters were there. I broke down and cried terribly when, after an hour, I did not see any sign of them. I was inconsolable.

Miraculously my mother survived. She was brought in on a stretcher two hours after I arrived. She weas unconscious. I cried as I looked at her face. She must have lost a lot of blood from a big wound on her side.

A FLASH FLOOD SURVIVOR SPEAKS

When she woke up, she threw her arms around me and wailed like a baby.

"Thank you Lord!" she shouted.

"Did you see your father and sister?" she queried.

"They are alive," I told her. My answer, though not founded on reality, was instinctive. Feeling hopeful, she got up but we did the not see my father and sister.

When we got back to the main island where our house used to stand, we also did the rounds of all the funeral parlors in the city. They were not there.

My mother broke down from such desperate news. My sister has not seen the beauty of the world, and yet she is gone. My father is also missing.

I still pray that one day both of them would appear, maybe during my graduation, my birthday or my mom's birthday.

My mother is trying her best to control herself. She said repeatedly that if my father and sister do not appear on my graduation day a few years from now, she would take her own life.

It is so hard to lose a father and sister to the storm and the flood. I decided to focus on my studies and continue praying for strength to carry on.

Jede Jean Aureo

Citizens, rich and poor alike, are always the victims in a disaster. The government and the private sector have been conducting disaster preparedness and risk – mitigation programs in earnest. In fact, several types of disaster survival trainings had been run for communities and individuals alike. However, there are social and economic forces that challenge these well – meaning efforts. Among these are urbanization in coastal regions, environmental destruction, illegal logging and mining, uncontrolled building of structures along river banks and improper waste management. All of these contribute to the factors that worsen the effects of disasters.

UNPREDICTABLE DISASTERS

It was the day after a strong typhoon hit Metro Manila in 2013. As I lined up to order food at the lone fast food restaurant open in our area, there was a long queue. I have seen those sullen and shocked faces before. There was an elderly woman accompanied by her grandson, lining up to place her order. There was a couple, still obviously trying to compose themselves from the aftermath of the typhoon's brief but devastating visit.

I have seen worse scenarios before. In my long years with the military, we were tasked to mobilize civic group support during emergencies. The flooding in large parts of Metro Manila in 2009 caused damage that was far more deadly and widespread. As one of the worst floods that took the metropolis in decades, the swelling waters came quickly in the dead of night. Before they knew it, ordinary citizens already had water in their bedrooms and living rooms. Unprepared, they did not have time to gather their precious belongings. At that time, nobody believed that such a destructive flood, would spare no one, not even the rich.

But natural disasters are now regular and frequent, at least in our part of the world in Asia. Every year an average of twenty typhoons pass through the Philippine Area of Responsibility. Count in the occasional volcanic eruptions, earthquakes, landslides and floods and you have a full calendar of natural and man-made disasters, especially during the rainy season from June to November. Normal as they are, these deadly calamities still claim lives and property. The big question really is: "Can a family really prepare for them?" Having aided disaster victims, and in many ways being a survivor of these events myself, I realize that a family must keep in mind a few important lessons when an emergency strikes. As I have emphasized in my previous book, *"Philippine Jungle Survival,"* a life-changing catastrophe can happen to anyone, anytime.

Looking at those people lining up to order food and seeing the blank stares belying their shock, disbelief and perhaps inability to comprehend what they had just been through, I felt lucky that I went through military training. I therefore learned how to stay calm and think of what I need to do first. This is why I would like to explain and let others know the correct attitude and frame of mind one needs to survive a crisis.

THE CALM BEFORE THE STORM

Most people are caught unaware by a disaster because it is deceivingly calm before a ravaging storm arrives. Sometimes, people dismiss the light rains that precede a storm. Yet, it is always wise to be mentally prepared when signs of an impending storm or disaster come. The more aware you are of the first small signs of calamity, the greater the chances that you will react correctly when it strikes.

A father was celebrating his birthday with his family in 2011 in Northern Mindanao. Unable to hear the neighbors' warnings because of the revelry, flash floods soon came upon their house. The water rose quickly as the father brought his two children to safety. He went back to the house to save his wife, but the force of the raging waters proved too strong for both of them. Unable to hold on, they were swept away and their bodies were never seen again. Their children were orphaned.

You cannot be caught unaware of an incoming emergency.

HOTLINE NUMBERS

One of the worst mistakes you could make is to ignore warnings. Many deaths would have been prevented, had people along the projected paths of destruction listened and followed the instructions carefully.

Television and radio stations are the best sources of disaster-related warnings and preparations. Prior to a calamity, the media will have updated and accurate broadcasts. Heed these. If they advise you to evacuate, do so immediately. The active media Twitter sites are @gmanews, @ABSCBNNews, @News5AKSYON, @dzbb, @DZMMTeleRadyo, @Philippine Star, @inquirerdotnet, and @YouScoop. There are several more media Twitter accounts that you can discover.

Social media sites like Twitter and Facebook have communities that actively update developments and information on approaching storms, floods and other calamities. Subscribe to these crowd-sourced information providers. There are also responsive government Twitter accounts that you might find valuable. These are: @MMDA, @dost_pagasa, @NDRRMC_OpCen and @OfficialLRTA. Service companies that have active Twitter accounts are: @meralco, @nlextraffic, @ManilaWaterPH and others.

Citizens' groups also maintain hashtags that you must remember. These are the following: #FloodPh for updates on

Always react to the warnings from community leaders and the media.

heavily flooded areas, #RescuePH for rescue needs, #TracingPH for locating missing persons and #walangpasok for class suspension announcements. Together, these information could prepare you to handle emergencies, especially those in Metro Manila.

Here are some useful numbers to remember:

- NDRRMC.................................(02) 912-2665
- AFP...0917-531-6972
- PNP...117
- Bureau of Fire Protection (NCR)...(02) 729-5166
- MMDA.....................................136 / (02) 882-415-77
  local 337 (rescue)
- DPWH......................................(02) 304-3713
- Philippine Red Cross...................143/(02) 527-0000 to 95
- PAG ASA..................................(02) 433-8526
- Philippine Coast Guard................(02) 527-3877
- PHIVOLCS...............................(02) 426-1468 to 79
  local 124/125
- DSWD......................................(632) 931-81-01 to 07,
  local 426
- DILG..925-0330
- Rescue 5...................................922-5155

Always monitor media alerts about impending disasters.

DANGERS WHERE YOU LIVE

To prepare yourself for any disaster in your area, you must know the types of hazards that may come.

Be acquainted with the history of earthquakes, flooding, landslides and other calamities in your area. You must know if your home and community are flood-or landslide-prone. Find out if your area is vulnerable to storm surges. The more information you know about the vulnerabilities of your area, the better prepared you will be.

Check the "Geohazard Map of the Philippines" at this website http://essc.org.ph. If you live in an industrial area, know the businesses, factories, warehouses, waste treatment disposal facilities and storage areas that can cause fire, chemical spills and explosions.

Be warned if your home is along a riverbank, creek or coastal area. These are most often vulnerable to flooding and storm surges. Beware if your house is on a slope, cliff or foothill. Heavy rains for a day or even just a few hours can trigger rockslides, mudslides or landslides down your way. So know the general layout and topography of your area and never be complacent.

Before you build your home, know the history of calamities in your dream location.

To prepare for an evacuation, have your survival kit always ready. The following are top priorities:

a.) **Printed phone numbers of family members and other loved ones.** In case you have not backed up your contact numbers in an online storage you will need the printed numbers.

b.) **Cash and ATM cards.** Banks will be closed and ATM machines non-functional. You must have hard cash for emergency purchases for medicines, water, food clothing and transportation.

You must have cash prepared to handle an emergency.

c.) **Identification Cards.** In case you are lost or anyone of your family members is missing, he can always show his identification card to rescuers.

d.) **Documents and Passports.** It is absolutely necessary to safeguard these documents. These must be placed in a waterproof bag and placed inside a backpack that the father must carry.

e.) **External drives and USBs.** We often pack our most valuable images and copies of our most precious works in external drives. If you cannot email these to yourself or have these stored online, make sure you wrap these in waterproof plastic bags before you head out.

f.) **Jewelry pieces.** You do not want these hard-earned treasures to be taken away by the flood or calamity. Make sure, these are stashed in a bag that you can quickly put into a backpack that the mother may carry in an emergency.

g.) **Records and certificates.** You must secure copies of your medical, dental and insurance records to bring with you. While you can obtain duplicates of these from the government agencies and corporations, the process may take time. It is best if you have the original copies with you.

h.) **Medicines.** One of the best things to prepare for an emergency are medicines for common illnesses that affect your individual family members. If you have children, you must prioritize your stock of fever, diarrhea, coughs and colds, hypertension medication. You must also have anti-tetanus, anti allergy, antibiotic and anti-leptospirosis medicines. You must also have your stock of the prescription drugs that your family members are required to take. You may have to stay at a place that is far from a drug store. The worst thing that can happen is for one of your family members to have a medical emergency.

It is important to have the essentials prepared before a disaster strikes.

i.) **First aid kit.** You must also have alcohol, band-aids, tweezers, absorbent dressings, bandage scissors, hydrogen peroxide, cold compress and a thermometer. In addition to these you must have sanitation kits to include tissue wipes, sanitary napkins, diapers, toothpaste, toothbrushes and soap. Bring plenty of anti mosquito lotion to ward off the insects.

j.) **Jackets and blankets.** Make sure that you bring along hooded jackets or raincoats to protect you from the rain and cold. If you have space, bring blankets that will comfort you and keep you warm. If there is space and you have infants or elderly, it also becomes important to bring pillows for them.

k.) **Extra clothes.** You will need to change clothes. In the case of extreme emergencies, shops will be closed for the first few days. Bring clothes, extra underwear and socks to make your life less miserable.

l.) **Water.** You will not survive your first three days out of your home without potable water. Make sure that each family member brings her own water container. You must carry water enough for a whole week.

Water and a battery-powered radio are very important for your survival.

m.) **Food.** Bring as much food as you can. Carry those that need not be cooked. Bread is an excellent carbohydrate source that can last for five days. There are also packaged cupcakes and pastries that last for months. Cookies and biscuits are useful too. Pack your bag with chocolate bars and candies to maintain sugar in your body.

Carry non perishable canned food that can provide you with protein and energy. If you are a mother with young kids, make sure to have chocolates and other foods children love. These would make life out of the comfort of your home more bearable for them.

YOUR EMERGENCY SURVIVAL KIT

In an emergency where you will have to evacuate, there will be no chance to cook. You would be lucky if you find a room in a hotel where there is food. However, it is always possible that you will find yourself in an evacuation center, just like everybody else.

My experience in disaster relief assistance proves that delivering instant noodles instead of rice is more advantageous. The refugees do not have pots and pans, let alone gas ranges. Thus, cooking rice and other viands was not even an option. However, instant noodles that need only hot water is an easy choice.

Prepare ready-to-eat foods to bring with you if you evacuate your home.

n.) **Batteries and flashlights**. In every emergency, there will be massive brownouts. Bring with you long-lasting batteries for your flashlights and radios. It is best to have rechargeable flashlights fully charged always. These come in handy when emergencies arise.

o.) **Battery-powered radio**. Do not forget to bring a small battery-operated AM radio to keep you informed of public service announcements, emergency updates and warnings.

Your car can be your second home if a disaster strikes and destroys your house. One of the best ways to prepare your car for an emergency is to fill it up with gas. If you have spare gas containers, fill these up as well. In disasters, huge traffic jams will occur. Thus, everybody will be lining up for gas and if their car runs out of gas, they will just flee and leave these on the road. You do not want this situation to happen to you.

Stock up on survival items inside your car trunk. A full trunk can last for a week. Have your flashlights, tents, food and other supplies inside your car.

Make sure your battery works and the ignition system is perfect. You cannot afford a major car malfunction in an emergency.

Park your car away from power lines and trees. You do not want fallen branches and electric poles damaging your car. To prepare you to leave with your car, park it where it cannot be reached by water. Make sure it is facing the direction you want to exit to. The confusion of people in an extreme emergency may rattle you. Plan ahead, decide how to move the car with your entire family in it. Plan your escape route well. Take note of potential flood and traffic areas along your planned route so that you do not get stuck like everybody else.

Have your car ready to escape from an emergency.

SAFEKEEPING YOUR DOCUMENTS
AND PICTURES

One of the worst things that a disaster can do is destroy all our precious mementos, documents and other possessions. Countless families lost all their pictures and documents in floods.

With the availability of video and photo sharing social media sites now, it is advisable to post copies of your precious documents and images online. That way, if flood waters rush through your house or strong winds carry these away, you will still have digital copies available online.

One of the best ways to weather-proof your original documents is to place them in waterproof plastic bags or containers. Nothing can substitute for the original copy of your diploma or award, and the only way to safeguard these in your homes is to have an easily accessible container to place all of these to protect them from the elements.

Digitize your documents and place these in waterproof plastic bags.

Should you be forced to evacuate your home in a disaster, make sure you prioritize moving out your precious documents first. While clothes and food are important, documents cannot be easily replaced or purchased like food and clothing.

Every disaster brings power outages. The heavy winds in a storm will wreck electric lines. Posts will fall, and wires will break. Because of the widespread devastation, the electric utility companies will not be able to respond quickly to all concerns. Thus, it is important to brace for brownouts.

Every disaster affects power services, so be ready for brownouts.

Should you have children and elderly in your abode, it is best to move to a nearby hotel immediately. They are often too frail or innocent to comprehend the effects of the disaster. Besides, the children and older folks might not be able to bear the discomfort of having no electricity at home.

During brownouts, it is also important to cook every perishable item in the refrigerator. The disturbance of agricultural and meat supplies could make vegetables and meat scarce or at best, too costly. Cook your stock and be ready to eat them on a scheduled

PREPARE FOR BROWN OUTS

basis.

Without electricity, water will be in short supply. If you are in the city, stock up on water. Buy water stocks in the groceries and water refilling stations. Conserve water during the crisis. You would not want to see your children suffer and be thirsty because you failed to adequately store potable water for them.

Your gadgets can help you survive in an emergency. One of the first ones you might want to have is an inverter. This device sources power through your car lighter socket. Since there is widespread power outage for the first one or two days after a storm or calamity, your car inverter will power your portable AM radio, laptop, portable Wi-Fi connection and even charge your cellphones.

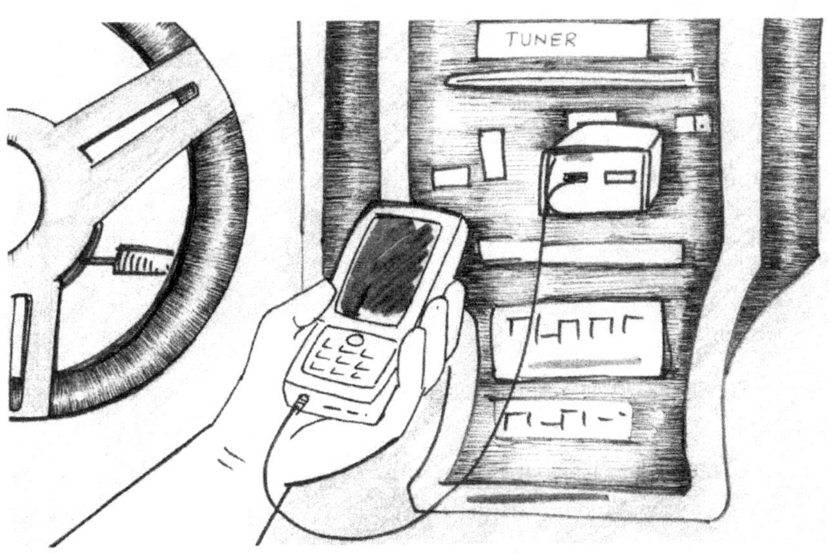

The inverter is a valuable tool during brownouts.

You must be aware of reconnection or other power-related emergency services of your electric distributor. For MERALCO customers, their hotline is 16211 or 0920-971-6211.

COMMUNICATION DURING EMERGENCIES

Power outages are bound to happen with strong winds. Since telecommunication companies are highly dependent on power, chances are high that internet and mobile services will be interrupted. In this scenario, it is very important to have alternative means of communicating with family members.

Have spare batteries for your cellphones ready. If you can afford it, buy portable battery chargers for your mobile phones. There is simply no substitute for a fully-charged phone in an emergency. Communication is most important during these times. During the massive metro flooding in 2009, I received a frantic call for help. One victim was trapped in his attic and had only a few minutes of cell phone battery power left. He was desperate for a rescue mission. We were able to rescue him because he had the presence of mind to call before his battery ran out.

Mobile phones are absolutely necessary. Just make sure to put all of these on econo mode so that you are able to conserve battery power. Better yet, purchase an older model of a mobile phone, which has minimal capabilities. These usually have a longer battery life.

You must have alternate ways of communicating with each other in case a family member gets lost.

WATERPROOF BAGS

During floods and typhoons, it is important to waterproof your precious gadgets, clothes and documents.

For your clothes, the most cost-effective means of waterproofing these is to wrap them in trash bags. Tie the top and secure with tapes before you leave your house. No misery can match being in an evacuation center without money, food and dry clothes.

Make sure to place your valuables into waterproof bags.

Mobile phones and gadgets are safe in water repellent bags and waterproof cases made especially for divers and mountaineers. These are designed to float for extended periods of time. Buy one that is designed exactly for the size of your phone, tablet or laptop.

If you have no access to these specially-made waterproof bags, simple plastic bags will do. Have ample allowance so you can tie the top of the bag tightly.

02

WHEN A DISASTER COMES

PARENTS DURING A DISASTER

A calamity that suddenly strikes a comfortable home causes panic among its members. Yet, it is very important that the parents maintain a calm demeanor, so as not to affect the psychological disposition of the children. While it may be time to panic, a parent cannot show it to her children because she will have a far bigger problem controlling them if she does. She cannot be hysterical because her children will see it and start to be afraid, even paranoid. Every parent must be calm even in the face of an extreme emergency.

One of my friends was only three years old when the destructive earthquake hit Baguio City in 1990. When the powerful earthquake struck, he and his playmates were outside their home playing. Too young to know, they even enjoyed the shaking of the ground and their playground. They were happy to experience such a unique feeling because that was the first time it happened. They did not know that the tremors destroyed sixty percent of the buildings in their city and brought instant death to many.

His mother was calm and collected throughout. Though she knew the extreme danger that her family was in, she did not show fear. Her husband was away and she was left to hold the family together. She was stable as a rock.

After the earthquake, she braced her kids for the aftershocks. She did not allow any of them inside their house. If they needed to change clothes, she would go into their house herself and get the clothes. They did not sleep inside their house for several days. His mother never showed any fear. In fact she just let them play and follow their normal routine. His father arrived a week after, when the roads to Baguio have been cleared for travel. And just like my mother, she calmly decided to bring her family down to Pangasinan, where there would not be any reminders of the earthquake.

Twenty six years later, when he was already a parent, he remembered the same lessons that his parents taught him. A strong typhoon hit Baguio City again in 2009. There were landslides in many places. And just like when he was a kid, food was scarce because all roads leading to the mountain city were closed. Just like the earthquake 26 years before, there was no electricity and the city market felt like a ghost town.

Every parent must be prepared for a disaster.

But his priority was keeping his child calm the way his mother did when he was young. With only candles lighting their house, he played games with his son. His son enjoyed the games without realizing that those games were played to remove his discomfort from the massive power outage. During the day, without TV or access to gadgets, father and son just played around with toys. In the end, his son did not feel the effects of the typhoon because he showed no fear. It is from parents that children pick up the best disaster-coping behavior.

Households where the father works away from home, only have the mother to shepherd her children during a calamity. It is during these times that she rises above her fears to protect the family. The next story comes from a grateful daughter whose mother saved them from harm. Without the heroic acts of their mother, they would have all perished.

OUR MOTHER, OUR HEROINE

I will never forget the day Typhoon Reming devastated Daraga City in Albay in 2012. To this day, I still carry the trauma of that experience. I thought it was the end of the world.

Typhoon Reming was said to have been one of the Philippines' ten most destructive typhoons ever recorded this century. We prepared for the worst, especially because lava flows passed our way whenever Mayon Volcano erupts. We have undergone drills and disaster preparedness exercises and even went through simulations. What we were not prepared for was the strong typhoon that would trigger lahar flows.

Indeed, when the typhoon came, we did not know what to do. The winds were too strong and the rains too heavy, we could barely see beyond our windows. We are used to typhoons but this was definitely the strongest. We huddled together in a room at the corner of our house. Without our father, we all felt helpless. But the howling winds soon ripped our roof off the house, exposing us to the rains. We had to seek shelter at a relative's concrete house.

Our mother showed courage as she saved all of us.

OUR MOTHER, OUR HEROINE

We all agreed we would all be safe there. However, that house was 200 meters away and getting there proved to be traumatic! My father was not around, so my mother braved the strong winds and everything else it took with it: pots, pans, radios and galvanized sheets. She first accompanied my little siblings. I kept praying that she'd make it safely back. Even I was too young then to help her.

Meanwhile, our neighbors were also asking for help. We could not do anything as we too, were fighting for our lives. My mother came back, bleeding. She stepped on a glass fragment from a broken window that lay on the road. She continued moving us out of our house, going back and forth despite the heavy rains and gusty winds.

Back and forth she went and when almost done, we became aware of another danger that threatened us. The heavy rains and strong winds had taken its toll on the volcano crater. Though we knew it was not about to erupt, we could see that lahar had begun to flow. We were told that it was going to be deadlier as lahar was heavier than water and could bring with it debris from houses that lay on its path. We knew there would be rocks and other volcanic material flying in all directions. We were lucky to have had sufficient shelter.

My mother was our heroine. Bruised and wounded, she continued walking back and forth amid rushing waters and strong winds until she had taken all of us, her children, to safety. She risked her life for us.

When we were finally able to leave our relative's house, we saw hundreds of bodies lined up at the public park. Huge trees were uprooted. Billboards and steel trusses lay twisted. Power lines went down with the winds. We knew recovery would take months.

We prayed and thanked God for having kept us safe and for our brave mother who was willing to risk her life for us.

Ms Rona Lobos

COMMUNITY PREPAREDNESS

Proactive measures save lives. Realizing the impending damage from super typhoon Yolanda in 2013, the municipality of Diot in Cebu would have suffered many casualties had it not been for one leader who forced the people to evacuate. Diot lies along the coastline and was right on the path of the supertyphoon Yolanda.

With the help of other leaders in nearby communities, warnings were relayed to the townspeople who promptly cooperated and moved to safer ground. They had adequately prepared for the typhoon when it came, so there were no casualties.

It is a leader's duty to heed such warnings and convince his constituents to evacuate as soon as possible, just as it is the duty of every citizen to cooperate, especially in times of emergency.

The following story highlights the importance of acting on evacuation warnings, despite our attachments to our material possessions at home.

HEED WARNINGS

In 2009, one of the worst floods to hit the metro came overnight. Our house was along the river in Montalban in Rizal province. There were early warnings that a flash flood would come raging fast once the water from the Angat Dam overflowed and the Marikina River reached dangerous levels. In fact, our village authorities came by a few times, warning us to evacuate.

Many among us, in the communities along the Marikina River, did not believe the warnings.

"Do not worry about it," one of my neighbors told our *barangay* leaders.

"We do not want to leave our houses and appliances," protested another.

Despite the orders of our leaders, many of us turned a deaf ear. They left, disappointed at our stubbornness.

The raging waters came a few hours after. At first, nobody could believe the volume, depth and force of the waters. It is as if, an entire dam had erupted and all its water came our way.

With floodwaters getting deeper, I rushed my nephew into safety.

I rushed to pick up my 2 year old nephew who was left in my care at that time. Luckily, we had a neighbor who had a three-storey house. I went back for another round to pick up his milk and clothes. By that time, the water inside our concrete house was already waist deep. When I went back again to gather food for my nephew and myself, the water was already 10 feet deep. I went back to the three-storey house, frustrated at not having brought back food.

For the next three days, we endured the lives of flood refugees. We called for rescuers but nobody came. We survived on what was doled out to us by the very same leaders whose warnings we ignored. By the time we went back to our houses after three days, we were all speechless, shocked at the utter devastation we saw. The very same houses we tried to protect were all under mud and water. Our television sets were floating and so were the refrigerators. Everything was damaged beyond recovery.

I saw the pathetic faces of my neighbors who were as sad as we were. They could not believe that one night of torrential rains could trigger such a destructive flood.

We were just lucky that nobody died among us. Had we listened to our leaders, we would not have lost all our possessions to the floods.

I learned my lesson that year: always listen to disaster warnings.

Noel Abdon

LOCAL CRISIS MANAGEMENT

In the chaos and confusion of an extreme emergency, there must be order and leadership. Without a single command and control, it would be hard to coordinate the well-meaning efforts of those who want to help. It is therefore important that victims, rescuers and first responders have a simple organizational structure to synchronize all the initiatives. Without crisis management, the confusion will lead to inefficiencies at the expense of the victims needing help.

While there are clearly defined incident command systems, local personalities can have different ways of conducting disaster relief, rescue and rehabilitation efforts. Therefore, the existing disaster management cluster in every region, province, city or town must convene regularly to plan and coordinate.

Each stakeholder has a unique contribution to play in any emergency. It is very important for each stakeholder to understand each other's expectations. This will clarify things so that when the calamity unfolds, things will be performed according to expectations.

There must be a strong local disaster management team to handle any crisis.

AFTER THE DISASTER

COPING WITH POST DISASTER TRAUMA

Among the hardest to manage after a disaster occurs are trauma victims. Often, they keep all the sadness and misery to themselves until they could not take it any longer. In the course of my work in disaster relief and rehabilitation for the Armed Forces and its partner organizations, I have come to meet many victims of different ages, means in life and backgrounds. Most of them present a stoic face, even a happy one. But once they start to narrate the sad tales of the disaster that struck them, they break down. The suddenness of the tragedy and pain of losing loved ones and possessions are just too much to bear.

If you happen to be a friend of a survivor, help her share her story, her pain, her agony. The more she shares these with others, the more she releases the pain from her system. This process then relieves her of the stress of surviving a major calamity and living to tell her tale. Let her cry. Let her express herself. Let her freely put out the pent-up feelings inside. If you are her shoulder to cry on, do not expect that the process will be short. Especially if she lost loved ones, the healing process will be long. Bear it out because it is never easy to lose loved ones to disastrous events.

The loss of loved ones and properties is hard to bear for calamity victims.

Life is hard after a disaster. This next story comes from a victim who had to spend difficult weeks in an evacuation center.

LIFE IN EVACUATION CENTERS

I consider myself lucky, despite the tragedy that befell our family. We lived in a small village by the river in Cagayan de Oro. We knew that there was going to be a flash floods when it rained hard nonstop for several hours.

Our family made the right decision to leave our house immediately. There was not much emotional decision-making because we only had a few possessions to speak of. Thus, we hurriedly left our house by the river. By the time raging, muddy waters came rushing down, we were already on a safe slope. It was a pity that we saw several people upstream struggling for dear life as the river tossed and turned them around in its mad dash to sea. I saw several people drown.

We headed straight to the village evacuation center, the school house. Though I was used to poverty, I never imagined how difficult

We had to dig root crops around our evacuation center to augment the relief goods delivered to us.

Philippine Red Cross
  (Port Area)   (02) 527-0000
DSWD National Resource
  Operation Center   (02) 851-2681

Foundations and government relief agencies are conduits of Filipino generosity to victims.

DELIVERING RELIEF GOODS

My extensive experience in coordinating relief operations logistics between the Armed Forces of the Philippines, the Red Cross, the Department of Social Welfare and Development, ABS-CBN Foundation and GMA Kapuso Foundation made me realize the logistical nightmare of delivering the precise number of the right type of goods to the right people at the right time.

One of the things I noticed, however, was that transportation assets are most needed in the days immediately after a disaster.

DELIVERING RELIEF GOODS

Trucks, especially wing vans, are most needed at this stage. Since it is most likely that rains will continue, wing vans are perfect for transferring and delivering relief goods like coffee, sugar, canned goods, water, rice and instant noodles. In my experience, I have observed that jeeps, vans, buses and trucks are more needed than cash at this stage. The warehouses of these organizations are usually overflowing with goods that cannot be delivered.

The logistics of delivering the right volume of relief goods on time is daunting.

These organizations are often undermanned and lack the transportation assets to deliver the goods. Most of the time, they approached us, the Armed Forces, to use our trucks, ships and aircraft. For inaccessible areas, Philippine Air Force assets are very valuable. The Villamor Airbase and Clark International Airport become the hub of relief operations when tragedies strike remote, isolated areas. Philippine Navy ships are also indispensable in bringing bulk relief goods supplies to affected areas.

04

THE FIRST RESPONDERS

DISASTER HERO ANYONE?

Nothing strikes more fear in the heart of a doting parent than the possibility of putting his or her children in harm's way. I have faced this unnerving situation before. But my wife has done so even more. In many instances, she has had to cope whenever disaster struck. I was often away on military duty and she would be left alone with the children. Many times, she would recount her experience when an unusually strong typhoon struck and she was alone in the building where we lived. She was pregnant with our child at that time and was really worried about what could happen. To this day, announcements of oncoming typhoons bring back those memories. She admits she was afraid, but because she did what was right when those disasters struck, she was able to protect our family. In that sense, she is a hero.

You can do a lot to help others during a disaster. Often, people will be weaker and may not be able to get out of a flood. Others will need emergency medical aid. Somebody will be in danger of drowning. Look out for these opportunities to save others. While you must not harm yourself when you do, the life you save will be good karma.

Many more heroes emerge during extreme emergencies. Many of them are mothers who instinctively take care of their kids, even putting their own lives on the line. Many are also fathers who would do anything to protect their brood. But there are a few who rise up to the challenge, face the odds and become disaster relief heroes.

One of the few that I have come to know became one of the unsung heroes in the wake of the flash flood that struck the Northern Mindanao City of Cagayan de Oro in 2011. This is his story.

THE LIFESAVER

I just got out of hospital confinement in Manila when typhoon Sendong flooded our city of Cagayan de Oro in 2011. One of my friends invited me for coffee. I was just happy to call it a night when we parted ways a few minutes after midnight.

As I was heading back to our house near the mighty river, I was shocked by what I saw. The water level was rising fast and people were screaming in panic.

"It must be a flash flood," I thought to myself. The people in my city had not seen a flood for generations. They did not know what to do. They were panicking, screaming at the top of their lungs.

I had to react. I went back to the house of my friend which was near the river. I knew it was in the path of the flash flood.

"Get up on the roof," I shouted in the dark. By the time I got to the vicinity of my friend's house, the water level had gone up quickly to 10 feet. I knew from previous disaster relief and rescue trainings in the military that it was just a matter of time before the water level rose even further.

I first assisted the elderly to safety.

The people were helpless. I first assisted the elderly up on roof of the house. It was the highest and probably the sturdiest among the houses in a lower middle class housing area. Then I went for the children. They were too afraid to climb the roof, so I told them to step on my shoulders to get them up.

DISASTER HERO ANYONE?

"Do not be afraid," I assured them. They simply could not comprehend what was happening and how it would affect their lives and loved ones. By that time I already had 15 of them on that roof.

"I have to go back and get my money from my store," requested a lady storekeeper. I did not allow her to go back.

"You will die if you do," I told her.

There were just too many within the immediate vicinity of my friends' neighborhood shouting for help. What I did was to improvise. I found a refrigerator among the floating objects. I took out the refrigerator door and I used it as my flotation device. Riding on it, I went to a neighboring house that was about to topple and dragged toward the sea. I even rescued a newborn and his grandmother.

Because the water level was about to hit the roof of my friend's house, I went for a few more of the neighbors to pick them up.

I saved 35 people during that flood in 2011.

By that time, I gathered 35 hapless victims onto a roof. But, the water kept rising. Instinctively, I knew that the 35 people may still get swallowed by the flash flood. Then I spotted a big log among the floating debris. I swam out and with all the force I had left, I secured the big log to the side of my friend's house. I planned to make it the Noah's Ark for the 35 people I had saved in case I had to move them out of the roof.

We must rise to be heroes during emergencies.

The people I saved were cold and frightened. Most were crying because they lost their loved ones. A few more hours passed, dawn broke, and the people I saved had to take in such a horrible sight: so many dead among the debris. There was mud all over the streets. The houses that had been unlucky got crushed and toppled by huge logs that came down.

"Thank you sir," a young college student told me.

"Without you, I would not be able to take my nursing board exam today," he shared.

I could not believe what he was telling me because despite his experience, he held on to his dreams. I did not know if the scheduled exams were even going to push through that day after all the damage that had happened.

DISASTER HERO ANYONE?

I was too weak to respond to the "thank you's" and praises from the 35 people I saved. Duty done, I casually walked back to camp. My clothes were full of mud. None of the taxis I hailed bothered to stop to pick me up. But the 16th cab did.

"Where did you come from?" the taxi driver asked.

I barely answered. By the time I got to camp, my superiors had heard of my noble deed. They gave me a plaque of commendation for exemplary acts during a crisis.

"I was just doing what needed to be done sir," I told my commander.

"The people you saved thanked you so much," my commander told me.

I never expected anything in return for my heroic act. Lives had to be saved, and I simply had to respond and do the right thing.

Master Sergeant Eddie Viador

Sergeant Viador's story of extreme heroism shows how deep conviction could translate into courageous action to save others. While this is not expected of everyone especially those who are not naturally inclined to do such selfless acts, there are indeed scores of unsung heroes who exhibit the inherent goodness of men and their willingness to sacrifice for others.

The main point that I wish to make is that heroism is inherent in all of us. A mother following her instincts would protect her children and keep them from harm. She would put everything on the line to save them. Extreme emergencies need people like her who would go the extra mile to save others. Many lives are saved this way.

It is often this willingness to lend a hand to one who desperately needs help that defines the true character of real heroes.

DISASTER PREPAREDNESS TRAINING

Sufficient knowledge and proper training lessen vulnerability to disasters. Disaster awareness trainings teach people to take the dangers of frequent disasters seriously.

Local governments have taken the initiative to conduct disaster training among their constituents. It is important that every citizen, no matter how comfortable their lives are, take these trainings seriously.

There are always disaster response volunteers helping out during disasters. The military's manpower and transport assets are always ready when disasters occur. There are citizens who help their local governments contain emergencies. Thus, it is important that local government leaders inspire their stakeholders to make their communities disaster-resilient.

Every community needs a group of disaster rescue volunteers.

The following story of a band of volunteers highlights the importance of these citizen groups.

VOLUNTEER RESCUERS

Together with few other mountaineers, we founded the Tanay Mountaineers in 1997. We have always wanted to use our skills and

VOLUNTEER RESCUERS

training in scaling mountains, first aid and survival for humanitarian assistance and relief operations.

Our first major test came in the wake of the landslide in Infanta and Real in Quezon in 2004. With our own personal protective equipment, we gathered ourselves and went for the first big test of our organization. The massive landslide along the road to the coastal towns rendered it impassable. Thus, we disembarked and decided to walk the rest of the way.

As we walked, mud clung to our boots. I realized that the landslide would not have happened had the trees not been cut by the illegal loggers. These irresponsible loggers had been cutting even the small trees. Whatever plants were left could no longer hold the water heavy rains brought.

As we walked towards the towns affected by landslides, it dawned on me that the very livelihood many people depended upon was what caused the landslide! It was during these moments of reflection on our way to the rescue site that I realized how important environmental protection was to preserve lives. We simply had to plant more trees and take care of our environment, the way we take good care of our families.

In every major disaster, there is always a need for rescuers. Trained rescuers who use their own equipment and spend their own money and time are not very common. That was what our group did. Our first test came when we retrieved bodies, helped victims trapped in their houses, repacked relief goods and distributed these to the households. It was tiring work but definitely one of the most fulfilling that I have ever done in my life.

The work of disaster relief volunteers comes in spurts. That is why we always have to be ready.

Our mountaineering skills were tested next. We were again deployed during the 2009 floods that hit the Metro and its environs. Our first appreciative customer was an elderly man whom we saved from the fast rising waters as he lay helpless inside his house. We

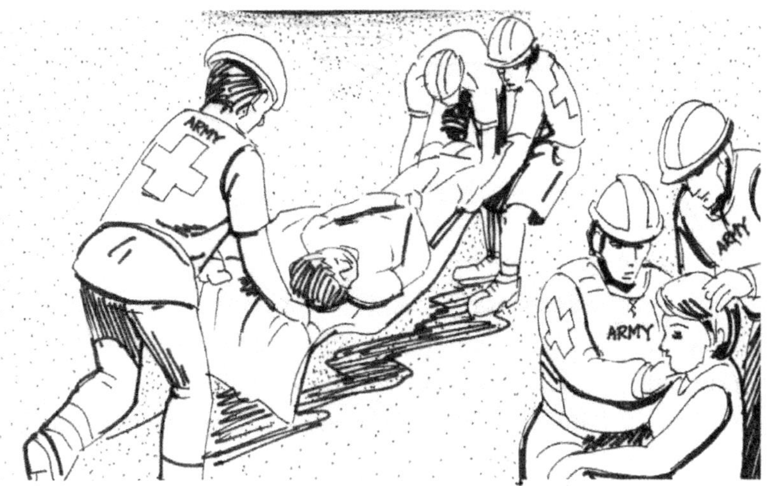

Volunteers like us risked our lives and used our personal resources
to save others.

then shifted our attention to a bunch of youngsters who were all on top of a fragile roof about to be taken away by the muddy and fast – moving floodwaters. We rescued them right before the roof of the house they were on caved in due to the strong current. We would not have been as efficient in our rescue efforts had we not been trained and motivated.

Since we founded our rescue volunteer group almost two decades ago, we have seen the greater awareness of people and local governments in disaster preparedness. We have volunteered to share our expertise in these trainings sponsored by government agencies, NGO's and other organizations.

I am just so happy that we have inspired other groups to form their own rescue teams. With the right attitude and training, they will also help other people in distress the way we have and find the same fulfillment when we founded our all volunteer disaster rescue group.

Engineer Carlos Inofre

FIRST RESPONDER EQUIPMENT

Whether you are an ordinary citizen called to become a first responder, a trained rescue operator or a soldier, you must have basic equipment in order to effectively respond. These are the practical and essential equipment you need:

a.) **Rope**. A long mountaineering rope is essential for a first responder team.

b.) **Megaphone**. You need a powerful megaphone to relay your instructions to victims. Some of them might be trapped underground, or under collapsed buildings. They would not hear you if you do not use a loud megaphone.

c.) **Chainsaw**. Especially needed during storms, landslides and earthquakes, the chainsaw is invaluable in cutting fallen trees blocking the roads.

d.) **Flashlight**. You need a powerful flashlight, as powerful as the ones miners use, when looking for victims in the dark. Since there will be brownouts during calamities, the flashlights would come in handy. Make sure to bring spare batteries.

Every first responder must be well-equipped to save lives.

e.) **Spare communication equipment**. With simultaneous requests for help, your cell phone battery will run out of power fast.

Make sure you have a spare cell phone and spare batteries.

There will be a breakdown in commercial communications infrastructure in major catastrophes. If you have other radios that do not depend on the telecom networks, you will find these very useful.

f.) **Rubber boat**. During floods and typhoons, rubber boats are indispensable. These can deflate when punctured by pointed debris in the water. Thus, any boat, especially with a fiberglass body, will be a good substitute.

g.) **Extra food, water and money**. If you are sent as a first responder, you cannot rely on anyone else for food and water. You must bring biscuits and water to fill you up. You will be too busy rescuing others that you will not have time to cook.

h.) **Extra clothes**. You need extra garments to replace your wet clothes.

i.) **Body bags, gloves and gas masks**. Gloves and gas masks are especially important because once you stay for more than 2 days in a calamity area, the stench of the dead will be unbearably strong. Have bags or blankets to wrap them with.

But perhaps, beyond the necessary equipment, you must have the spirit to save your fellowmen. It is a difficult job to rescue others because you yourself are in danger, regardless of how well-trained you are. You must be ready to give it all you've got in the service of the unfortunate disaster victims.

As a rescuer, you must be prepared to handle extreme situations.

DISASTER MEDICS

A medical team is very important during catastrophes. One of the most common cases during a calamity is high blood pressure. People break down under the sad rush of events. They need medical assistance fast.

Patients would also come in, bruised from debris. Some would also come with broken bones. These cases need immediate attention.

During storms and floods, there are cases of victims feeling very cold from hours of exposure to the rain and winds. There are also cases of people needing resuscitation. Fainting from the pressure of the tragedy, they lose consciousness. They need expert medical attention to regain consciousness.

In floods and storm surges, there are also cases of drowning. Every medical responder must know how to administer cardio-pulmonary resuscitation to unconscious drowning victims.

It is therefore important that people attempting to rescue others must have basic first aid knowledge. But most importantly, the presence of medical professionals in extreme situations is absolutely necessary.

Medical professionals are urgently needed during disasters.

In every major catastrophe there will be death. It is important that early on, you know that the smell of rotting corpses and decaying carcasses are part of a post disaster scenario.

As a parent, it may be hard for you to make your children understand that death is part of a calamity. Yet, you must tell them, because such is the reality of total destruction. Their trauma will linger if they do not understand the scenes of dead victims after a disaster.

The smell of decaying human flesh is offensive. In fact, it takes getting used to. Wear a gas mask. If you have medical gloves with you and you are part of the retrieval operations, make sure you wear latex gloves before you handle a decomposing corpse. If you do not have any chemicals with you, at least bring alcohol and chlorine that you could pour over the corpse to lessen the stench.

The odor of decomposing animals is as strong. Make sure you bury these immediately to prevent any diseases from spreading to the living.

Pray that you will be able to handle human corpse retrieval operations because this is one of the worst tasks after a catastrophe.

The strong odor of decomposing corpses is unbearable to survivors.

The following story is that of a young soldier who responded to the gory challenge of corpses retrieval operations.

MY FIRST TEST

I was barely three months in the Army when my first real test happened. It was not about hunting for the enemy deep in the jungle. It was not about firing cannon rounds into enemy camps. My first test came when a flash flood ravaged several communities in our area. Our mission was to save as many as we can in the village that was worst hit.

I was shocked by the tragedy. Almost everybody in that community perished. There were layers of corpses piled one on top of another. A child hung on one tree branch, lifeless. I could not imagine how miserable he must have been as he fought for dear life in the raging waters. I could not bear the sight of death.

Retrieving corpses was indeed a very difficult job.

I spotted another dead child, with one arm torn off by some violent force. His body was stuck in a railing. Though the water had subsided, it took a lot of effort for me to take the little corpse out.

"Be strong," commanded our platoon leader. He too, was holding back his tears. Among us, he was the most personally involved. He grew up in that place. He knew he was about to break down but as a true leader, he did not.

We searched for survivors in the mud, the slushy mud that had taken thousands of lives in that tragedy. We did not see any. Most were buried deep in the mud. A few hours into our retrieval operation, we already counted 53 corpses.

"Focus on the job," our leader inspired us. Yet there was something so gory about everything.

It was December 16, and with Christmas fast approaching, I could not feel the merriment of the Yuletide season. I was among the living in the village of the dead.

I could not feel the hunger and the fatigue. I could not feel thirst as we methodically picked up corpses from among the ruble. In fact, I had a duty to do and there was something about picking up a lifeless body and lining all these bodies up that affected my inner being.

"Don't use your heart. Rely on your mind and your training," commanded our officer as he discovered yet another corpse in the mud. In those circumstances, using one's heart and becoming captive to one's emotions would surely cause a break down.

It took us almost three days to complete our mission. By that time, the stench of decaying human flesh was too strong and weakening. Yet, we managed to do our duty. Though weak and thirsty from the intense days of retrieval, I learned what service to fellow-men truly meant. I realized that to be a soldier is not just a job. It is a total commitment to help others in need.

Private Frank Mapano

Despite the extreme circumstances that every calamity brings, nothing compares to the power of prayers. It is in calling God when we need Him most that we find strength to weather any storm. The following story comes from a survivor of the strongest super typhoon to hit the Philippines so far.

volved. He grew up in that place. He knew he was about to break down but as a true leader, he did not.

We searched for survivors in the mud, the slushy mud that had taken thousands of lives in that tragedy. We did not see any. Most were buried deep in the mud. A few hours into our retrieval operation, we already counted 53 corpses.

"Focus on the job," our leader inspired us. Yet there was something so gory about everything.

It was December 16, and with Christmas fast approaching, I could not feel the merriment of the Yuletide season. I was among the living in the village of the dead.

I could not feel the hunger and the fatigue. I could not feel thirst as we methodically picked up corpses from among the ruble. In fact, I had a duty to do and there was something about picking up a lifeless body and lining all these bodies up that affected my inner being.

"Don't use your heart. Rely on your mind and your training," commanded our officer as he discovered yet another corpse in the mud. In those circumstances, using one's heart and becoming captive to one's emotions would surely cause a break down.

It took us almost three days to complete our mission. By that time, the stench of decaying human flesh was too strong and weakening. Yet, we managed to do our duty. Though weak and thirsty from the intense days of retrieval, I learned what service to fellowmen truly meant. I realized that to be a soldier is not just a job. It is a total commitment to help others in need.

Private Frank Mapano

Despite the extreme circumstances that every calamity brings, nothing compares to the power of prayers. It is in calling God when we need Him most that we find strength to weather any storm. The following story comes from a survivor of the strongest super typhoon to hit the Philippines so far.

FLOOD

TYPES OF FLOOD

I actively participated in building schools and distributing relief goods in the aftermath of typhoon Sendong in Northern Mindanao in 2011. The 10 hours of torrential rain triggered deadly flooding that claimed more than 2,000 lives in the cities of Cagayan de Oro and Iligan. Overnight, water level rose by three meters and higher, causing landslides and disastrous flooding.

Flooding occurs when heavy rains last for a few hours or more. It could also happen when a dam overflows and dikes and levees give way. Storm surges could also drive high coastal waters, thereby causing flooding in seaside communities.

There are different types of floods. Based on location or place of occurrence, there are three types. The first type, urban flooding, occurs in cities where the urban sewerage system and

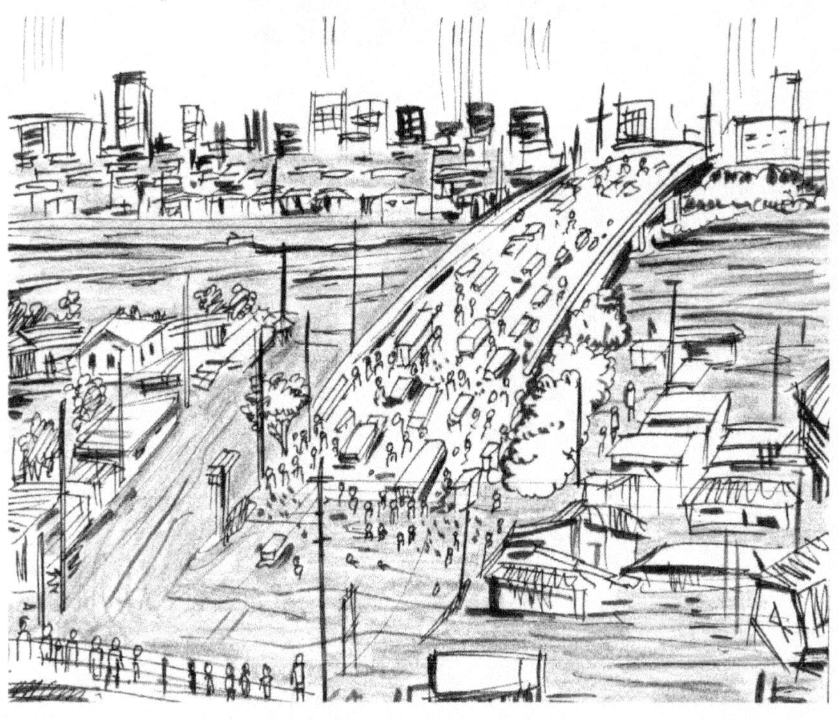

Tropical storm Ondoy in September 2009 brought a month's worth of rain in 12 short hours, flooding Metro Manila.

concrete structures are unable to absorb the excess water brought by heavy rains. The water that is not absorbed by the ground is retained in the surface and accumulates to become flood water. Coastal flooding, on the other hand, is caused by a storm surge, tsunami or high tide coinciding with heavy rains. Tsunamis caused by waves produced by earthquake tremors are as dangerous as storm surges. Storm surges occur when strong onshore winds push the water inland, thereby flooding the low lying coastal areas. The third type, river flooding, occurs when excess water from the rains causes a drastic rise in the river levels.

Based on duration of occurrence, there are two types of floods: sheet flooding and flash floods. Sheet flooding is normally shallow water overflowing from river channels and dams. Flash floods are different. There are flash floods in mountainous areas or in steep places that have rivers in between the mountains. This flash flood occurs when there is unusually heavy rainfall in a concentrated area. Flash floods become dangerous because of the landslides that these create. With huge amounts of water dumped onto a mountain system that have no trees to retain the mountain soil, landslides occur. When mud and soil push their way into the river system, the combination is forceful enough to wreck the houses on the river banks.

Factors that contribute to flooding include denudation of forests and watershed areas. The spate of flooding and landslides all over the Philippines are greatly the result of uncontrolled illegal logging in our forests. Garbage in rivers also make these shallow, thereby lessening their draining capacity. The abuse of building codes which give rise to non-compliant buildings and houses also contribute to flooding. Much of the flooding in urban areas is also caused by malfunctioning drainage facilities. The spread of informal settler colonies along flood plains and river banks also greatly induce urban flooding.

MOVE TO HIGHER GROUND

In an impending flood, one of the best things to do is to go to higher ground. If you are in the city, start scouting for elevated areas. In every subdivision or village, there is higher ground that you could head off to. If your house has a second floor, move there. Bring along your valuables. The flood level in your house could rise in a matter of minutes. Do not wait until water is waist-deep before you relocate. By that time, it may be too late.

The best option in the city is to move to a building or even a mall. These can shelter you and your car during the flood. Be wary, however, as the elevator eventually malfunctions in a high rise building. You might find yourself stuck for several hours or days before the electrical system is fully restored.

If you are in the rural areas, and there is threat of a flashflood, head to high ground immediately. Stay there until the rains are gone and the flashfloods have subsided. In a flood, never take refuge along rivers streams, creeks and canals. Move up a hill, away from any body of water. You will be safe there.

Move to higher ground quickly once flood warnings are announced.

You can survive a flood if you have the quick survival instinct to secure a flotation device. Old tire interiors are useful. Inflate these as soon as there is a warning. Styrofoam containers or ice boxes are always handy flotation devices. An old, non-functioning refrigerator is one of the best flotation devices. You can place an infant or a child inside so it functions like a raft. You can also use big pails and basins as flotation devices. Keep these within reach and when the floodwaters come, these can be very useful.

Being caught in raging currents of flash floods is very dangerous. If you have the strength, head for the river banks immediately. You do not want the water bringing you out to sea.

But if you are caught by floodwaters, your journey throughout the length of the wild river will be wrought with danger. You might hit a rock in the middle of the river. You might get slammed by logs and tree branches. There also sharp objects like metal or bamboo sticks that can pierce your body. These are extremely dan-

Find anything that can serve as your flood raft or flotation device.

WHEN CAUGHT IN FLOOD WATERS

gerous. If you have the chance, hold onto a branch along the river bank. Use all your might to get out of the water if you can. But if the river current is too strong, grab a flotation device immediately. The best are floating logs, large pieces of bamboo or banana trunks, iceboxes or refrigerators. These are good flotation devices.

One of the flash flood survivors I have come to know was a thirteen-year-old girl who survived by clinging to a log. In 2011, she found her house being steadily flooded in the middle of the night. Being made of light construction materials, their house was flushed away by the strong river current. She and her siblings saw themselves floating but surviving in the rampaging river waters, until they bumped into a bridge. Though hurt from her collision with the concrete bridge she and her siblings found logs stuck under the bridge. She grabbed one and held onto it, until she fell asleep from exhaustion. A few hours later, she found herself marooned in the island of Camiguin, a few hundred kilometers from her home in the Northern Mindanao City of Cagayan de Oro. She never found her siblings and parents but she was lucky to have survived by floating on that log.

There is another story of a miraculous rescue of a baby by placing him in a pail during a dangerous rescue that involved crossing a wild river.

SAVING A BABY

At the height of typhoon Yolanda's fury, many soldiers were deployed to save families isolated by rising flood waters. A few families who have made their home under a bridge were trapped on one side of the riverbank.

A team of Army rescuers learned of their plight and set out to rescue them. It was a difficult challenge because the water was so deep and dangerously fast. It was hard to cross and wading through was not an option. They made a two-rope bridge after several vain attempts to establish a foothold on the far side of the river bank. The lead man of the Army team was actually wounded as he braved the raging waters to establish the rope he carried.

Seeing the first soldier reach the victims was like a miracle. The first one he rescued was a two-year old baby. He put the baby in a pail and guided it across the river. It was one of the most delicate actions he had done in his career. One false move and the baby drowns. As the soldier carried the other victims to safety, they realized that the people did not have much choice. These were poor families and vegetables were their source of livelihood. They needed to stay near the river for irrigation.

Having rescued them gave the soldiers joy and satisfaction.

It was a miracle to have saved a baby placed in a pail.

The preceding story highlights the hard choices that poor families must make. They either build homes in high risk areas near their livelihood or go hungry. Most of the time, they have no other choice but risk it all than die of hunger. Local leaders must consider removing their residents from possible harm to guarantee adequate sources of income.

SHALLOW FLOOD WATERS

After a flood, water may stay for days or even weeks until these totally drain out to sea or to the river. Children love to frolic in flood waters. There are several instances where they play around in knee-deep floods. But shallow flood waters are dangerous and neither you nor your children should wade in them. It is never advisable to wade, much more play in flood waters because of the dangers lurking in these.

Snakes, big and small, abound during floods. Driven off their habitat, they also struggle to survive. They will readily bite you if you step on them.

You can also get punctured or lacerated by sharp objects in the flood waters. There are broken glasses, rusty nails, metal fragments and even syringes.

If you have open wounds or skin rashes, it is also dangerous to wade through the flood waters. These are teeming with bacteria and contaminants that can cause diarrhea or leptospirosis.

Do not allow children to play in shallow floodwaters.

KEEPING YOURSELF HEALTHY AND WARM

During the continuous rains immediately before or after a flood, drying clothes is difficult. If you live in the mountains and do not have access to warm jackets, plastic sheets will do. Wrap yourself with a plastic sheet, like a trash bag. This will trap the heat of your body. If it is really very cold and wet, chew on a tobacco leaf or betel nut. These would keep you warm.

Continuous rains and flooding will challenge your health. Your continued exposure to dirty flood water may cause athlete's foot and acne. To prevent this from happening, clean and dry your feet and then wipe oil onto the soles of your feet. This layer of oil should protect you from dirty water.

The cure for ringworm, skin allergy and athlete's foot are boiled guava leaves applied over a period of several days. Another method of treating these foot problems is to grind garlic and spread the paste over the infected area of your feet.

Wrap yourself with garbage bags to keep you warm.

RE ENTERING YOUR HOME AFTER A FLOOD

As you pick up the pieces, be very careful when go back home. Go inside your house with a flashlight. Refrain from using torches or lanterns, because these might ignite flammables that may have leaked inside your house while you were gone.

Be alert for hazards when you enter your house. Most dangerous are snakes and centipedes, so watch out for these. There may be broken wires and exposed, live ones. Do not touch any electrical appliance if the floor is still wet or if you are standing in water. Check for fire hazards. Dry all wet electrical circuits before turning the main switch on to ensure that you do not get electrocuted. Have an electrician check your house before you turn on the main breaker.

Do not try to fix things on your own. Report any damage to electrical, water, gas and telephone lines to the service utilities or to your local government leader.

Hungry and thirsty as you may be, refrain from eating any of the food left inside. These might have been contaminated by the flood waters.

WHAT YOU CAN DO TO REDUCE FLOODING

As a citizen, you can do a lot of things to reduce your community's vulnerability to flooding. You can help dredge and declog city rivers and tributaries. You can help in reforestation and watershed management efforts. You can help in easing the urban drainage system by helping remove obstructions in drainage channels. Together, you and your community can reduce your vulnerability to floods.

TYPHOON

TROPICAL CYCLONE

The Philippines is often described as "Asia's Typhoon Mat" because the seas around us spawn regular, destructive typhoons. Our country has the highest frequency of tropical cyclones in the world. An average of 20 tropical cyclones hit the archipelago each year, each one categorized according to its strength or intensity.

Disastrous cyclones ravage the Philippines regularly.

CLASSIFICATION OF TROPICAL CYCLONES

There are four types of tropical cyclones. These are set by the speed of the maximum sustained winds near the center measured in kilometers per hour (kph).

Tropical depression - 35 kph to 63 kph

Tropical storm – 64 kph to 117 kph

Typhoon – more than 118 kph

Super typhoon – more than 220 kph.

When the onslaught of a low pressure area or a typhoon is broadcast, pay attention to the flight path of the developing storm. Though the path may change at the very last minute, it is important to note which part of the cyclone would hit your area. This should better prepare you.

There are three parts of a cyclone, namely: the eye, eye wall and rain band. The eye is the center that is circular in shape. With a diameter ranging from 10 to 100 kilometers, there are no clouds, only light winds and no rain.

When the eye of the storm passes over an area, there is a lull lasting a few minutes to an hour. The eye wall causes the heaviest damage when it passes over land. The strongest winds are on the wall of the storm. The rain bands are made up of rain and thunderstorms surrounding the eye. Rain bands bring heavy downpour and high wind gusts.

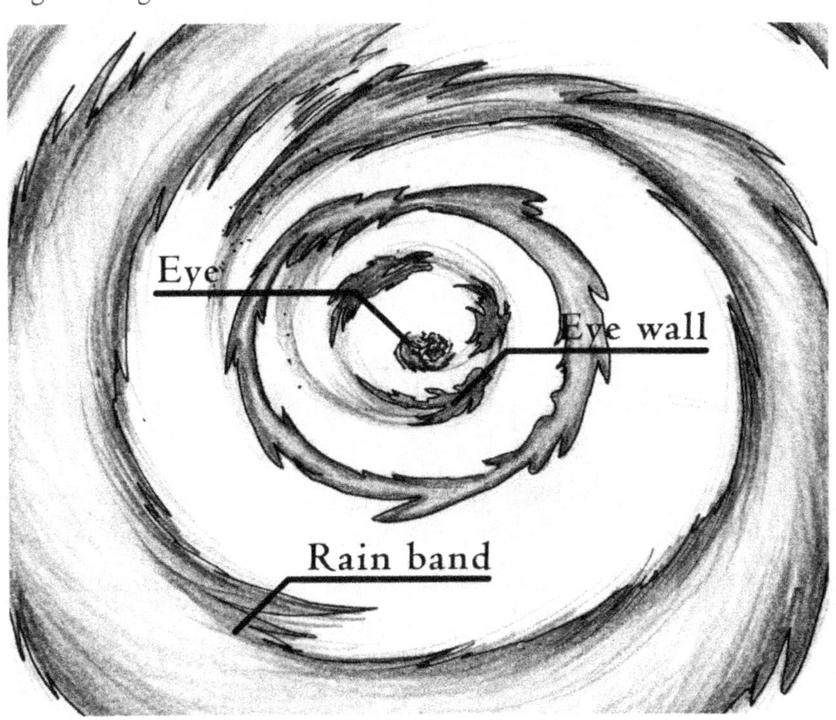

Know which part of the typhoon will pass your area.

PUBLIC STORM WARNING SIGNAL #1

This signal is raised when winds of 30 to 60 kph are expected within at least 36 hours. Intermittent rains may also be expected within 36 hours. Very light to minimal damage is expected. However, plants which are at their flowering stage may be affected. Business is as usual and outdoor activities are not cancelled. Classes do not need to be suspended.

A Signal #1 storm does not cause significant damage to properties.

PUBLIC STORM WARNING SIGNAL #2

For this storm warning signal, winds from 60 kph to 100 kph are expected within the area in at least 24 hours. Because the storm may intensify and possibly change direction, the public is cautioned not to take unnecessary risks. Sea and coastal waters are dangerous to small seacraft. Outdoor activities, especially those of children, must be postponed. The strong winds will affect rice and corn plants. Banana trees will be bent and may fall. Coconut and other trees may also fall or be uprooted. Business signages may fall. Shanties may be destroyed. Classes may be suspended during Storm Signal #2.

PUBLIC STORM WARNING SIGNAL #3

During a Signal #3 storm, people must already evacuate to high and strong buildings. They must likewise flee low-lying areas and stay away from the sea shore and river banks. Rough seas and coastal waters make traveling with any sea craft dangerous. Winds greater than 100 kph are expected within the next 18 hours. Agriculture will surely be affected. Houses of light or medium construction are damaged. Coconut trees may fall and banana trees may be uprooted. There may be widespread disruption of power and communication services. Classes at all levels must be suspended and work may be suspended as well.

A Signal #3 storm damages houses, livestock and agriculture.

PUBLIC STORM WARNING SIGNAL #4

A Signal #4 storm indicates that extensive damage to the community is likely. All travel by land, sea or air must be cancelled. Evacuation to sturdy buildings is strictly enforced.

Since very strong winds of more than 185 kph are expected in at least 24 hours in the community, this will be a very strong typhoon that will cause a heavy toll on the community. Electrical power and communication services will be cut. Buildings and houses may be damaged.

A Signal #4 typhoon can bring unimaginable destruction to hapless victims and their property. Thus, it is very important that every one appreciates its power to destroy.

Some survivors of the Signal #4 super typhoon in 2013 are still unable to come to grips with the worst experience they had been through. The following is one of the thousands of stories of hope and revival.

A SUPER TYPHOON SURVIVOR SPEAKS

Even before the typhoon came, we were already instructed by community leaders to move to the big church in our town, Carigara, Leyte. Our family decided to move to the smaller church where we belonged, although it was not made of materials as strong as the big church.

On the day Typhoon Yolanda arrived, my father refused to leave our house. "I do not want to leave our small store," he declared. I was crying because I knew that it would be dangerous for him to stay. My mother, nine siblings, my two children and I lived in that house too.

"These material possessions would not mean anything if we lose you!" I told my father. I begged him to leave with us, but he was adamant. "The Lord will protect us all," he calmly replied. His tone was reassuring, so typical of the devout. He assured us that nothing would happen.

I was really worried. I was the eldest and some of my siblings were the same age as my own children. The thought of losing my father to the typhoon bothered me.

We left him and two of my brothers there while I herded the rest to our little chapel.

The rains came first, then the wind got stronger and stronger, beating at our makeshift chapel. We prayed together in the main prayer room until the howler came upon us with all its might. The galvanized iron roofing broke free of its trusses first. Only then did

I learn what "howling winds" really were and how it felt to be so exposed.

My mother and siblings began to cry. I, too had begun to be afraid as we had little protection from flying debris.

"Lord, please keep my family safe," I murmured, just as the last remaining piece of roofing was blown away. It felt like the typhoon's rage was focused on us. Shivering and wet in that roofless chapel, we clung to each other and prayed for safety. By the grace of God, the typhoon left a few hours later. When we got out of that small room, we saw the damage caused by Yolanda. The typhoon leveled our entire town, leaving electric posts twisted and houses destroyed.

After surviving the super typhoon inside our chapel, the twelve of us thanked God for keeping us safe.

We thanked God that we survived but we were worried about our father and brothers who were left in our house. We rushed to them and found them all alive. We were so grateful for having been one of only a few families without casualties.

A SUPER TYPHOON SURVIVOR SPEAKS

As we surveyed our village, the destruction was indescribable. Whole houses were washed away into the sea. People cried, confused and at a loss as to how and where to start rebuilding their lives. Our possessions were also damaged but not as bad as theirs.

However, we had to find food. There were no stores and no supplies came in. We were all hungry. Relief goods came in the next day. My little siblings and my own children were only too happy for the warm porridge we were given. I did not mind giving up my share.

We prayed that more relief goods would come, but everything was rationed. Only one kilo of rice was allotted for each family. We were lucky to have had instant noodles and sardines, though rice was always wanting.

I took pity on my kids as they lost so much weight. When the flow of goods began to normalize, prices of meat and fish remained high. But there was nothing we could do as we understood that the merchants needed to recover too!

Eventually, I decided to leave with my two kids for Manila where my husband worked. It seemed to have been the only option for me and the others whose breadwinners were in Manila. I did not want to burden my parents as the relief goods they received were barely enough for them.

I was grateful that God kept my family safe. "We are survivors," I kept telling myself.

I am now safe in Manila. But every now and then, I feel guilty for having left my family, afraid that something may happen to them if another typhoon comes.

Unable to resume their livelihood, my parents could no longer put my siblings through school. I took them to Manila, hoping I could give them a brighter future. But deep inside, I know that the same thing could happen in Manila, or worse, an earthquake may bring destruction. I always pray that what had happened to us then will not happen again.

Criselda Goza

PREPARING YOUR HOME FOR EVACUATION

Never attempt challenging the power of nature. Even the sturdiest and most expensive homes can be wrecked by strong winds, raging water and shocking tremors. Be ready to vacate your home in an emergency, no matter how painful it is to do so.

Before you leave your house, make sure you prepare it for your departure. Shut off water and electricity outlets. First turn off the electric breaker and unplug all appliances. If you have time, move all your electrical appliances to a level safe from floods.

Lock your door and make sure to keep a separate set of keys for all the doors in your house.

Upon the warning of an incoming storm, trim the branches of trees beside your house.

MOVE OUT FAST

People can become attached to their material possessions - including the homes they saved for. Whether they are challenging or defying the odds, waiting for a miracle, or are simply in denial, they

MOVE OUT FAST

refuse to leave until the last minute. Many times, it is too late. This is the most disastrous decision that the family can make.

The weather agencies always give everyone a fair time to prepare for the onslaught of a calamity. Most fall victim to deadly disasters because they shrug these warnings off until it is too late to evacuate their families to safety.

While there exists a margin of error, these predictions and typhoon speeds and paths could change anytime. These typhoon warnings are fairly accurate. Listen to the weatherman's suggested precautions.

You do not want to be caught unaware when disaster strikes. A flash flood victim I got to know told me that his house made of light materials was washed away by fast-moving waters. Two siblings were taken away by the powerful current while another was unable to leave the room. He survived, but his siblings did not as they were not able to pry their doors open. It is important to leave as soon as one senses danger.

Move out of your homes before the full strength of the typhoon comes.

In this next personal narrative, I emphasize the importance of communication with family members in extreme emergencies.

WHEN YOU ARE AWAY FROM YOUR FAMILY

It is hard to be poor when calamities strike. I come from a farming family in the outskirts of Sibul, San Miguel, Bulacan. My parents do not have the basic necessities in life like a radio, television set, not even a cell phone. For us, having endured this kind of life for decades, we were thankful we were able to make ends meet. Yet, there was something different when typhoon Santi hit our village in 2013.

I was then a construction worker in a hardware store seven kilometers from our house. I took my bicycle to work, but that week, my boss asked me to work overtime. Then, at around 3 pm that day, severe storm warnings were issued in our town. The winds were so strong that the galvanized roofing of my humble quarters at the hardware started flapping noisily. Then the heavy rains came with the winds. In time, I was cold and miserable. Then it occurred to me that my family members may be in greater danger.

I knew that my family did not know the intensity of the

I never imagined that our hut in the mountains would be so completely
devastated by the typhoon.

storm. They did not have a radio or television. And there were no neighbors to run to for support. Even more alarming was that there was no way my family could contact me because they did not have a phone.

I wanted to run the seven kilometers home. But instinct prevented me from doing so. There was a total blackout. Galvanized roofings were flying dangerously. Steel and aluminum frames flew like crazy. It was too dark and dangerous for me to go home and risk being crushed by falling trees and debris.

Before dawn broke, I ran home to see my family. It was like an obstacle course among debris, and all other waste thrown haphazardly by the wind. I did not feel tired at all, despite running the full seven kilometers.

I was relieved when I saw my entire family all safe and sound. They were wet, cold and hungry but they found safety in a natural rock shelter near our home. Our house was completely destroyed except for the four posts still standing.

I just thanked God that nothing happened to them. I will buy a radio and maybe a television set when I get a better job. For now, I am happy they are all alive.

Gino Tagasa

As can be learned from the previous story, winds do the most damage to houses, buildings and infrastructure. Casualties come also from inland flooding and storm surges. Yet there are ways to escape the wrath of typhoons if you are resourceful enough.

Should you happen to live in the countryside where your fishing or farming village is highly vulnerable to a strong typhoon, one option is to head to the hills where you could be safe. The following story narrates a time-tested survival technique of a Samar-based family that had gone through years of surviving typhoons without losing a member.

TYPHOON FOXHOLE IN THE HILLS

Army sergeant Jaime Arceño had to let go of his dreams of finishing college when typhoon Undang ravaged their town in 1984. Having seen storms of varying strengths, to him, this was the strongest. He saw old coconut tree trunks get whipped, twisted and snapped by the winds. One of the worst things he saw in that typhoon were two people whose bodies got whacked and cut by flying galvanized roofing sheets as they ran for cover.

What has saved his family was something they had always done. Upon learning of a typhoon warning, they headed off for the hills that would not be prone to landslides and did not have large trees, only grass. They would then dig a 7 by 7-foot foxhole along the side of the hill, away from the expected direction of the wind. They then put simple roofing and stock on water and food. From the safety of these foxholes, they survived the succession of flood and typhoons in their disaster-ravaged province of Samar.

Their farmland did not, however, survive the storm. Left without any source of income, he was forced to quit college and work instead.

Building a foxhole on the side of a hill where there are not too many trees can save your family.

WATCH OUT FOR FLYING DEBRIS

The most dangerous things during a typhoon are flying debris. Twigs and branches of trees may fly off and hit you. The parts of houses built of light materials may peel off fast, and their old, galvanized roofing will injure you if you get hit. Even entire roofs may fly off with the wind. Thus, it is very important to stay indoors when winds are very strong.

If you really need to signal a rescue, put out a white blanket or any cloth of highly visible color instead. Write on these in big letters. Rescuers will surely see you. This method will have the same effect as going on top of your roof as doing so would put you at risk.

Flying debris are most dangerous during storms.

TYPHOON FIRST RESPONDERS

The first responders in the wake of super typhoon Yolanda in 2013 witnessed complete destruction. Arriving at the towns of Eastern Samar, Southern Leyte, Leyte and most especially Tacloban

City, utter chaos greeted them. Corpses lay on the streets and on the roofs while survivors desperately searched for their loved ones.

Those who managed to survive were in a state of shock. While they were used to typhoons, their province being within the typhoon belt of the Philippines, the devastation was simply unimaginable.

The wrecked structures, long believed to be strong, were no match to the fury of the storm surge brought on by the super typhoon. The transmission towers made of sturdy steel frames were twisted by the winds. Steel trusses from the buildings looked like twisties. Trucks, cars and vehicles were in complete disarray. Some were upside down, some were piled on top of one another, and all were destroyed.

But perhaps the one thing that no one there will ever forget was the stench of decomposing human flesh. It was so pervasive that it was at times disheartening. Yet despite all these, people helped one another and picked up the pieces.

The first responders at the typhoon Yolanda scene in 2013 could not imagine the destruction the super typhoon had wrought.

SEA TRAVEL

During the typhoon that ravaged Southern Mindanao in 2012, the path ran along the traditional fishing routes of tuna fishermen. Initially, hundreds of them were missing. By God's grace, many of them were saved. But we must remember that fishermen — or anybody else for that matter — cannot defy the forces of nature.

As soon as a typhoon or a storm enters the Philippine Area of Responsibility, the Philippine Coast Guard issues an order for all sea craft to heed their warning. Small sea craft are not permitted to sail once a storm comes in precisely because the risks are too high. Even medium-sized seacraft are not allowed to leave the port. Yet, many fishermen often defy such warnings and still head out to sea. They often end up dead or missing. Thus, it is important to heed the warnings of the Coast Guard during these times. You can contact the Philippine Coast Guard at (02) 527 3877 or at 0917 724 3682.

Fishermen must always heed the warnings of the Philippine Coast Guard, Philippine Navy and other maritime agencies.

MINIMIZING DAMAGE TO AGRICULTURE

Farmers are most prone to calamities. However, there are precautionary measures that they can do to preserve their fields and trees.

Rice and corn fields are often the most damaged. If you can harvest quickly, go for it. It is better to get a little from your labor than have nothing at all.

Trim branches and leaves of fruit-bearing trees, so that these will not be heavy. Mango trees, for example, are top heavy and are often uprooted by strong winds. Trim the branches so that the whole tree will not absorb the full strength of the winds. It is better to have your trees upright and with less branches, than it is to see your investment be swept away by the disaster.

Trim leaves and harvest ripe fruits of coconut trees. This way, you at least get something from your coconuts.

Banana plants cannot stand strong winds. Trim their leaves and harvest fruits before they are destroyed by the typhoon. Even the young bananas can be boiled and eaten.

PETS AND LIVESTOCK

In a storm or flood, your livestock will be as vulnerable as you are. If you rely on these animals for a living, make sure you secure them along with ensuring the safety of your family.

Cows, goats and carabaos must be brought up a hill where these will be protected by the slope. Tie them to a sturdy stake on the ground so that they won't flee from the flashes of lightning, the strong winds and heavy rains. Do not tie them under small trees that could fall and crush them.

Your children's pet birds must be left in their cages. Make sure you secure these so that they would not fly out. If you have pet dogs or cats, take them with you. Though you may not have enough time to take care of them as you fend for yourself during the emergency, these pets are like family members, so bring them with you.

PETS AND LIVESTOCK

Many of your livestock will not survive a storm or any other disaster.

LAW AND ORDER AFTER A DISASTER

The rule of law can break down when tragedy strikes. This is what happened in the aftermath of typhoon Yolanda in Tacloban.

Department stores and groceries were looted within the first few days of the tragedy. Television footages showed people carting away goods. People were desperate even for medical services. They would grab medicines lying around even if they did not need the prescription drugs. Yet law enforcers themselves were victims of the calamity and could do little because they, too, had to take care of their families.

Even the policemen brought in from other cities found it difficult to control the people. In the distribution of relief goods, for example, the people swarmed the choppers delivering the goods. Hungry and thirsty, they rushed for food despite the warnings from the policemen. It was a sad sight, indeed, but the tragedy was too great and civilization broke down. Order must still be kept even in extreme circumstances.

FINDING FOOD FOR SURVIVAL

It is impossible for relief workers to deliver all the goods that affected people need. The logistical requirements for moving massive amounts of relief goods are too heavy for the government and private transportation assets to simultaneously deliver. I have come to learn of this nightmare because with every major catastrophe, we had to assemble all the military trucks, the Navy ships and Air Force cargo aircraft to respond to the people fast.

Yet most victims were in areas not accessible by transportation and cut off from communications. There was simply no other way to reach out to them because we did not know where they were.

When typhoon Pablo hit the country in 2013, many of the isolated pockets of mining communities were completely cut off. With the devastating winds and heavy rains, they saved themselves by moving together to safer ground. But they became so completely unreachable that help did not arrive until a few days later. Many victims, even those affected by other calamities died waiting for relief goods to come.

Able-bodied members can remedy the situation. They can forage for root crops like yams and other tubers. These would not normally be affected by even the strongest typhoons. They can hunt and butcher the wandering animals that would by then be weak and confused. Even the rivers and creeks will be teeming with hungry fish and shrimp after a typhoon destroys their feeding grounds.

For water, the fallen coconut trees will yield potable coconut water and meat. The crown of the coconuts can also be cooked for nutritious meals. Of course you can always harvest undamaged bamboo shoots for hearty meals.

After a typhoon, there will not be too many fruits hanging on trees. Yet, you could always pick those that dropped on the ground. Unless these are overripe and full of worms, these are edible. These would give you the energy you need.

You will have to survive on your own if you get separated

FINDING FOOD FOR SURVIVAL

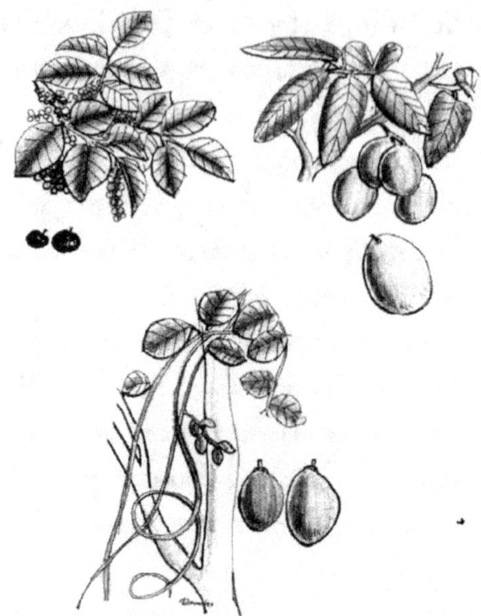

Even in typhoon-ravaged areas, you can still find wild fruits to harvest.

from your family members after a flood. If you find yourself in the mountains after a flood, trap animals. One of the easiest to trap is the monitor lizard.

If you live near the sea, there will always be seaweeds after a flood. Shrimps also abound after a flood because of the murky waters along the river banks. It is also easy to trap fish like milk fish, eel carp and other fish after a flood. Look for urchins among the rocks and the corals. These can be filling and stave hunger after a flood or heavy rains.

You should not just wait around while waiting for relief goods. Look for water, food and meat in the ravaged areas.

WATER, WATER

After any type of disaster, one of the major concerns is water. In an earthquake, the shocks and tremors will break water lines and even damage reservoirs. After a flood, wells and water supplies will be so severely contaminated to be considered safe for drinking. After a storm the dirty debris and garbage coming from all over will contaminate your water sources, including the clean rivers and streams. More so in a tornado where dirty objects can pollute traditional sources of water.

During these times, what is most important is not to rely on your normal sources of water until the situation has stabilized. Faced with a situation of producing water in the first few days after a disaster, the safest way is to get back to nature.

Coconuts can provide you with coconut water or milk to sustain you for a few days. Among nature's gifts, coconut water is one of the cleanest and safest to drink right after a calamity.

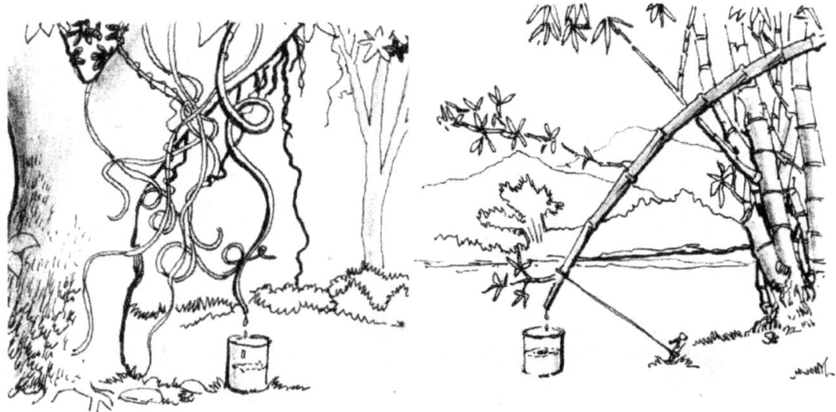

Tap water from vines and bamboos if you are in the countryside.

Water trapped inside bamboo can also come in useful. Water from vines can also help you if you really have no other source of water.

During this time, you must refrain from drinking from sources that you have always thought safe. Restrain your children from drinking tap water because they could easily get diarrhea. If there is really no other source of water, go to the relief agencies and for sure, they will have tons of mineral water for you and your family. Should you have a water refilling station in your area that runs water through several stages in filtration process, its source might not be as clean. Thus, be very careful about what you drink.

HERBAL MEDICINE AFTER STORM

Many diseases and sicknesses emerge and spread faster after a calamity. It is very important that you know a few things about herbal remedies, in case you do not find medicine. For fever, gather a cupful of *okra* seeds. You then dry-fry, grind and boil these, then drink the decoction. You could also finely chop 3 cups full *camias* leaves. Boil these with one gallon of water. You then apply this all over your body to relieve you of fever.

Against coughs, you can boil leaves of either the *lagundi, mansanilya* or oregano. Drink these for several days and your coughing should go away.

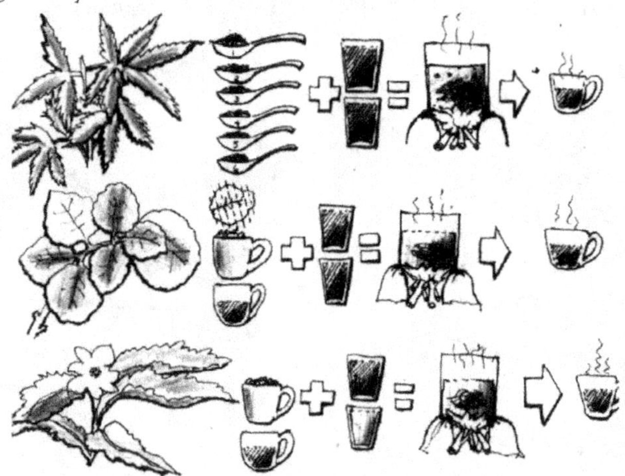

You can prepare the *lagundi* and oregano concoctions against coughs.

Against loose bowel movement, one of the most effective herbal remedies is boiled *kaimito* leaves. Just drink the decoction and your stomach trouble will go away. Even the *makahiya* leaves, finely chopped and boiled, are an effective anti-diarrhea remedy.

Against boils, the *gumamela* flower is effective. Pick a young flower, a bud. Cut a hole through a piece of cloth and apply this against the boil. Then put the young *gumamela* flower on top of the boil, right where the hole is. In three days, the boil should burst and release its "eye."

07

EARTHQUAKE

EARTHQUAKES

An earthquake is the violent or mildly perceptible shaking of the ground. Unknown to many, around 20 earthquakes occur in the Philippines each day. Though most of these are not felt, about two hundred earthquakes are felt every year.

More earthquakes are expected to come because our archipelago lies between two major tectonic plates, the Eurasian Plate and the Philippine Sea Plate that traverse the length of our country. The movements along active faults and subduction of plates along the trenches contribute to the abnormally high number of seismic activity in the Philippines.

Be prepared for the worst earthquake so that when it comes, you will know what to do.

PHIVOLCS EARTHQUAKE INTENSITY SCALE

There are ten degrees of intensity in the Philippine Institute of Volcanology and Seismology (PHIVOLCS) earthquake intensity scale.

Intensity I. Scarcely Perceptible. Delicately balanced objects are slightly disturbed and still water may move a bit.

Intensity I: This is a barely perceptible earthquake.

Intensity II. Slightly Felt. People resting indoors can feel this slightly but they feel no cause for alarm. Hanging things may swing slightly.

Intensity III. People residing in upper building floors will feel this. The especially sensitive people will experience dizziness and nausea, hanging objects will swing moderately.

Intensity III: People residing in the upper floors of buildings feel this minor quake.

Intensity IV. Dinner plates, spoons pots and kettles, glasses and windows will rattle. The floors and structures will start to creak.

PHIVOLCS EARTHQUAKE INTENSITY SCALE

This earthquake is felt by people outdoors and indoors. Though no considerable damage is expected, vibration is felt and a rumbling sound may be threatening to the public.

Intensity IV: Floors and structures will start to creak and people outdoors and indoors feel the shaking.

Intensity V. Within buildings, strong tremors awaken those asleep and some run outdoors. Hanging things swing violently and dining utensils clutter and clink. Damage may be seen in light to moderately - constructed buildings.

Intensity V: Strong tremors shake utensils and appliances. People are alarmed.

Intensity VI. Very strong shaking frightens people and some

lose their balance walking or standing. Heavy household objects may be displaced. Wall plaster may crack and poorly built structures are damaged. Rocks and boulders may fall along the mountain sides.

Intensity VI: People run outdoors and most lose their balance.

Intensity VII. Destructive – Landslides and lateral spreading of the ground may occur. Most people are traumatized and those indoors cannot stand due to the shaking. Heavy objects and furniture fall. Even well-built structures may be damaged.

Intensity VII: Walls may cave in and structures destroyed.

PHIVOLCS EARTHQUAKE INTENSITY SCALE

Intensity VIII. Very destructive. Concrete dikes are destroyed. The foundations of bridges are damaged. Utility posts and towers tilt or fall. Water and sewer lines are bent, twisted or broken. Landslides and rock falls occur. People panic and head outdoors.

Intensity VIII: Dikes and bridges crack and there is massive destruction of infastructure.

Intensity IX: Devastating. People cry and shake in fear. The trembling forces people to the ground. Buildings and concrete structures are badly damaged. Trees are shaken violently or fall. There is massive destruction.

Intensity X. Completely devastating. Most man-made structures are totally destroyed. Land forms are distorted and ground fissures develop.

There had been very strong earthquakes that devastated our country's cities. The magnitude 7.8 earthquake in July 1990 caused a 120 kilometer - long surface rupture. It also significantly damaged a 20,000 square kilometer area that included several Northern and Central Luzon cities.

METRO MANILA WORST-CASE SCENARIO

One of the greatest dangers posing a threat to a large part of Metro Manila is the Marikina Fault. Running almost parallel to the C5 circumferential road and going through a major commercial area and several residential subdivisions, this geological fault slips on the average every 310 years. When it does, the Marikina Fault delivers 6.0 to 7.0 – Richter scale strength tremors. The maximum estimated strength is 7.5 magnitude, which is devastating enough to destroy the structures along it and those very near the fault. It is estimated that the fault is not due to slip in the next fifty years or so, or about year 2064 or earlier.

If such a quake occurs, the National Capital Region, Bulacan, Cavite, Rizal, Western areas of Laguna and some areas of Pampanga and Batangas would be damaged.

There is massive devastation in Metro Manila if the Marikina Fault slips.

Should this happen, an estimated 30,000 people may perish, 2.2 million families may be displaced and would need food and shelter. Due to the widespread devastation, people will be severely

METRO MANILA WORST-CASE SCENARIO

traumatized. Basic services like electricity, water, transportation and communication will be disrupted. There might be a breakdown of law and order.

If this major quake does occur, wide open spaces like soccer fields and golf courses are safe evacuation points. The farther away you are from dense commercial centers during this time, the better.

In Metro Manila, major evacuation centers have already been designated. These are:

- University of the Philippines grounds
- Marikina Sports Complex
- The ULTRA in Pasig
- The AFP Golf Course and all other military golf courses
- Intramuros, if there is no tsunami.

These areas are expected to host tent cities and emergency medical facilities if this catastrophe happens.

What could make matters worse if this happens is when Manila-based staff of relief organizations are not able to report for work. Only 30% at most are expected to report for work while the rest would be ensuring the safety of their families, if not securing their own persons.

EARTHQUAKE RISK MAPS

One of the most important results of studying the potential destructive impact of a 7.2 earthquake came through a collaboration of several government agencies is a risk map showing potential damage and injury to people in Metro Manila.

To prepare yourself and your family for this gory scenario, you must follow disaster-resilient design, materials and construction of your house or building. You must be active in discussing local hazard maps with your community members and local government leaders. You must also faithfully comply with land use regulations and ordinances. These measures may just spare you.

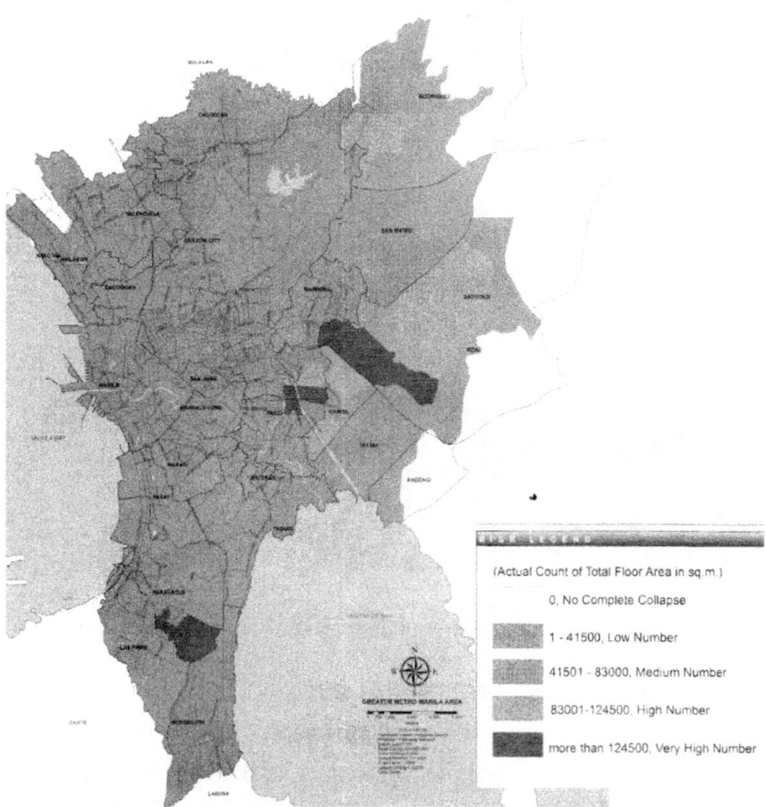

This earthquake risk map of Metro Manila is available at http://www.geoportal.gov.ph/.

BEFORE AN EARTHQUAKE

You can prevent some of the damage an earthquake brings. You will just have to make all the necessary preparations in your home or place of work.

For your home, you must secure hanging and breakable belongings first. Place latches on kitchen cabinet doors, especially the overhead storage areas to prevent their contents from falling or spilling out during the earthquake. Secure hanging objects like ceiling fans, and chandeliers which might fall during the earthquake. Fasten television sets and stereo systems to the walls or put these down to

Always know the hotline numbers of rescue agencies in your area.

the floor if these are not fastened securely.

Bring down your computers and microwave ovens to the floor and strap these to a stationary object like a post. This way, these would not be moved around by the shaking. Store all heavy items on the floor or on the lower shelves of your cabinets. Strap your refrigerator so that it does not fall and spill its contents. Strap heavy cabinets to the wall to prevent these from being toppled by the quake. Store your breakable objects and other kitchen utensils in a sturdy plastic box so that these will not break.

Finally, make sure that you disconnect flammable objects like LPG tanks from the oven range. This would prevent the possibility of fire. If you have chemicals in your house, secure these harmful things as well so that you reduce the possibility of damaging your home.

Listen to the radio or TV that might give you updated warnings about aftershocks.

These steps, if followed, should minimize the damage to your home.

THE DEVASTATING BOHOL EARTHQUAKE

The earthquake that hit Central Visayas in 2013 was the deadliest in decades. The energy it unleashed was equivalent to 32 Hiroshima bombs. Hardest hit was the tourist island of Bohol which, in 1990, was also hit by an earthquake and a tsunami. Although the 222 dead were not as high relative to the strength of the earthquake, damage to cultural and tourist spots was unimaginable. Centuries-old churches were violently shaken by the tremors. The famed Chocolate Hills, one of the main attractions of Bohol, were badly damaged. Roads and bridges were destroyed. It was indeed sad to see all the precious historical landmarks destroyed after centuries of preservation. But there is really no way we could control, much more challenge, the forces of nature.

Religious and cultural landmarks were totally destroyed by the strong earthquake in Bohol in 2013.

Most earthquakes come as a surprise. The following story shows how people who are caught unaware react.

AN EARTHQUAKE SURVIVOR SPEAKS

Nobody in our peaceful and quiet island province of Bohol foresaw that a strong earthquake would hit us. It had been generations since a quake jolted our province. Not even our grandparents have any memory of an earthquake.

"Run, run, run!" people were shouting. I could not believe what was happening. I was a member of a catering staff and early that morning, we were having our first cup of coffee when the tremors began.

The earthquake that came without warning shocked us to our senses.

My dorm mates and I did not know what to make of the forces shaking our fragile home. The tremors seemed to shake its foundations to the core. Our catering equipment were falling off shelves, wine bottles slammed against each other and cracked. Glasses and plates fell off the shelves, too. "Run for your lives!" shrieked someone. I did not know what to do. I must have stood frozen for an entire minute. When I came to my senses, I got out barefoot, numb with fear. Then, just like everybody else, I kept running helter-skelter. No place in Tagbilaran City seemed safe. I remembering muttering a prayer but what was stuck in my mind were the shouts of people who, like me, were also confused.

"There's a tsunami coming!" someone shouted. I was afraid because our dormitory stood near the sea. There weren't very many tall buildings in Tagbilaran to accommodate all the people. I knew I had to save myself, but I did not know how.

The major shocks left the city devastated. Buildings collapsed, stronger ones had cracks and foundations of some houses were damaged. Bridges broke apart like Lego toys and most damaged were the centuries-old churches that had been among Bohol's attractions. Those precious 200 – 500-year-old churches were no match to the 7.2 magnitude earthquake the shook Bohol.

I was lucky to have survived even the aftershocks. I also managed to control my fear. Just like others, I have learned to prepare for the worst. I now have a small bag filled with essentials I may need if another disaster strikes. Most of all, I have prepared myself mentally for any disaster that I pray will never come.

Ellen Mae Salva

EARTHQUAKE DRILLS

One of the best proactive things that a community or an organization can do to prepare for an earthquake is running earthquake drills. These drills encourage us to take earthquake precautionary measures seriously. These also practice us in what must be done when an earthquake strikes. Regular execution of earthquake evacuation procedures in critical facilities such as schools, hospitals, malls and areas of high people concentration may reduce casualties. The development of technical rescue skills among people may complement these drills. Rescuing people in collapsed buildings is very dangerous and requires great amount of skills.

DURING AN EARTHQUAKE

Your actions during an earthquake can save your life. If you are outdoors, move to a clear and open area fast. If you are out in the mountains or steep hills, move away from ridges, escarpments and cliffs. These might be affected by a landslide.

If you are near the seashore, head inland to an elevated portion. If you feel the earthquake is strong enough to prevent you from standing, assume that the tremor will trigger a tsunami. Go to higher ground fast.

If you are near a tall building, stay away from glass windows, walls, posts or other structures that might collapse. Beware of falling objects from the building.

If you are inside a structurally-sound building or in your house, avoid glass windows, large heavy cabinets, hanging objects or mirrors. Stay away from sharp objects with edges that might hurt you. Protect yourself by staying near strong columns or beams or outside the elevator shaft. Surfaces and architectural details are often the first to fall during a quake.

During the initial tremors of an earthquake, take shelter under a sturdy table or furniture.

Earthquakes come without warning. Thus, the sheer violence of the tremors give you only a few seconds to react. Practice the drop, cover and hold method to save yourself.

When you feel the earthquake, drop to the ground and crawl to a spot where you can take cover. Get under a sturdy table or furniture and stay there. Do not run outside or go to another room. Hold on to the legs of the table until the shaking stops.

If you are in bed when the quakes start, do not panic. Cover your head with a pillow, unless there is a heavy picture frame above your bed. Do not walk out through broken glass without your slippers or shoes on.

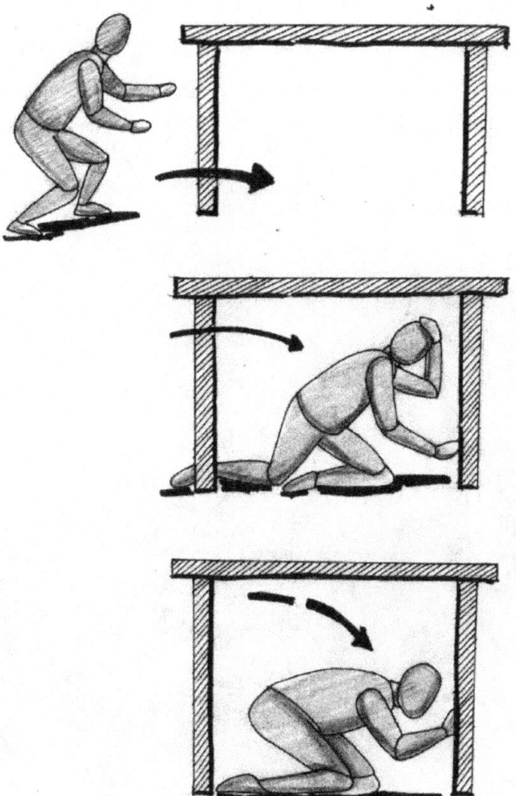

The drop, cover and hold technique is an instinct to practice for the coming of an earthquake.

This is the story of an earthquake victim whose family members all survived a strong earthquake.

WHEN AN EARTHQUAKE STRIKES

An earthquake comes unannounced at any time of the day. It comes in full force in any city or town. Our city of Kanlaon in Negros Oriental was hit by an earthquake in 2012. I was then just a normal teen in high school. But nothing in my previous experience could have prepared me for the utter devastation.

On the first major tremor, people in the streets panicked. Few have experienced the ground shaking the way it did. Some went running out, then into their houses. Some ran up and down the street. The first gruesome sight I saw was a woman whose leg slipped into a new crack on the road. Unable to pull it back out, her foot got crushed when the motion of the ground went in reverse — totally crushing her bones.

The houses were next to go. Those of light construction ma-

I never imagined the damage of an earthquake until I experienced one.

terials got destroyed like cardboard boxes. Some occupants did not have enough time to flee.

The buildings and houses that belonged to the rich merchants in our city cracked and some went down too. I discovered how buildings make a terrifying sound when they crumble as the ground shakes.

"Let's head for the mountains," ordered my father. He knew that we would be safe in the nearby hills which did not have big trees that could fall. We ran off to the hills while other relatives ran with us too.

It was a gruesome sight, seeing people crushed under the weight of fallen lamp posts and building beams. It was a gory scene. Yet we also had our own lives to save.

We did the right thing. Though we felt the aftershocks in the hills, there was no danger of erosion, landslide or falling trees. We barely had anything to eat or drink in the two days we sought sanctuary in the mountains but we survived the earthquake.

And I thank God for that.

Jhun Zaldy

AFTER AN EARTHQUAKE

Be extra careful after an earthquake. There are always aftershocks that might trigger the crumbling of buildings. Once the tremors stop, take the safest and quickest way out of the house or building. Do not enter partially damaged structures as these may collapse with the aftershocks. Do not use the elevators. Take the stairs instead.

If you have to re-enter your home immediately afterwards, do so with caution. Check your LPG tanks to make sure they will not explode. Check damaged wiring that may ignite. If you have not turned off your main electric breaker, do so immediately. Clean up dangerous chemical spills like gasoline, kerosene or muriatic acid. These might start a fire.

Carefully replace your displaced things in their proper places.

THE DESTRUCTIVE BAGUIO CITY EARTHQUAKE

On July 16, 1990, a strong earthquake measuring 7.2 on the Richter scale struck the mountain city of Baguio. Though other cities were damaged, Baguio was particularly hit hard. Since all three roads leading to the city suffered major landslides, access was only by air. Yet, the people prevailed.

The first 48 hours were particularly important. My Philippine Military Academy classmates all offered help. There were many people trapped in collapsed buildings. The cadets did their best to rescue the victims so that they could get immediate treatment. Injured victims were given first aid.

The cadets and the miners made their way to trapped persons stopping only when exhausted. After a few days of hard work, the cadets were happy to go back to the Academy knowing that they have rendered service when their countrymen most needed them.

Rescuing trapped victims is one of the hardest missions for earthquake first responders. This is the story of a heroic Philippine Military Academy cadet who, along with the Cadet Corps, rose to the challenge of rescuing victims under the rubble of the Baguio City earthquake.

RESCUE INSIDE COLLAPSED BUILDINGS

I have been through several major catastrophes in life. Typhoons, floods, landslides – I have seen them all. Yet, one of the most memorable was when I became one of the first responders in the massive earthquake in Baguio City in 1990.

I was then a cadet at the Philippine Military Academy when a series of powerful shocks rocked our world inside the Academy. Damage to some of our buildings was immediately evident. Luckily, we in the Cadet Corps were at outdoors formation then, so nobody got hurt.

RESCUE INSIDE COLLAPSED BUILDINGS

"Prepare to move!" announced the loud speaker.

"Get your mini shovels, flashlights and ropes!" ordered our cadet commander.

"We will rescue people in Baguio City proper," barked our leader.

We received no training as first responders. We did not know rescue techniques. But the spirit to help was strong.

A few kilometers from the Academy's gates, we spotted our first challenge. The buildings in the Baguio Export Processing Zone were in shambles. I could not believe the extent of the destruction. Concrete slabs were everywhere, piled one on top the other. The buildings had collapsed—totally.

As we got closer to the ruins, we heard faint cries for help from under the rubble.

"Help us, here.. inside!" came the cries for help. Acting on instinct and without care for my safety, I tried to find a way in. With

We saved many lives digging through the rubble after the Baguio City quake in 1990.

RESCUE INSIDE COLLAPSED BUILDINGS

my bare hands, I pushed furniture aside and after much effort getting past the dense debris, I finally got to where most of the trapped people were. There were many dead, many more were bleeding and most definitely, so much more were trapped elsewhere. The cries of those in pain echoed throughout the ruins. I struggled to regain composure, thinking of how we could quickly extricate the victims. There must have been more than fifty of them there. Luckily, one of my brave classmates also found his way in. Then we systematically moved out people from under the debris.

It was a challenge to do so, considering that there were several aftershocks. It was extremely dangerous to be rescuing people with the regular aftershocks, but we felt we just had to save the victims.

We made several trips out bringing the wounded and the living to safety. Every time we brought one out to the safe arms of our fellow cadets outside, we would see the faint smile of appreciation for the risk we took to save them.

On one trip back, we heard cries for help from one of the ground floor rooms of a three-story building.

"My hand is crushed! Help me!" cried a victim. When we found her, we saw how bad her situation was: her right arm was crushed by a steel beam.

"What do we do?" I asked my fellow cadet

The victim answered. "Just cut my arm off," she requested. Gruesome as it might have been, my buddy cut her arm with a Swiss Army knife because that was all we had. With a profusely bleeding arm amputated, we brought her out to safety. We were unable to save her arm, but we certainly saved her life.

Already tired after so many hours of rescuing victims, we heard another faint cry. This time, it came from the deeper corners of the collapsed building.

"Please come for me!" we heard her plea.

Again, I instinctively grabbed a flashlight and made my way through. It was dark and everything was topsy-turvy inside. Just being inside that collapsed building was dangerous. But it was impossible to ignore the call for help.

I found a female executive with her one foot trapped under the weight of a concrete beam. I first tried to pull her out but the weight of the beam would not allow me to. She was crying, bleeding, praying.

"Just cut my foot off," she begged me.

I did not know what to do because I only had a flashlight.

"I will call for help outside, ma'am," I re assured her. Luckily, better equipped rescuers had arrived when I got out of the building.

"Let us cut half her foot," advised the better trained rescuer that I led to the woman. The executive was shrieking the pain when we cut her foot. With all the blood coming out, it was a gory scene indeed.

As we negotiated our way back into the light, I carried the amputated lady on my back. Much to my surprise the President of the Philippines was there to greet us when we emerged from the rubble.

"Congratulations, Cadet Criste," the tobacco-chomping former general-turned – President praised me.

"You just saved the life of the General Manager of the Baguio Export Processing Zone," he declared. The loud cheers and thunderous applause of the people drowned my surprise.

The extreme fatigue from intense rescue operations came with accolades for our heroism during those critical hours. I got a Bronze Cross Medal for my feat. I was definitely one of only a few in the Cadet Corps given that award.

But to be honest, I was just reacting to my instincts. Something in our training in public service taught us about the willingness to sacrifice, at any price. The danger was there, but the desire to serve makes you accept the risks that accompany any emergency situation.

Major Isagani Criste

Earthquakes are few and far between but these are definitely destructive. This next story is from one who had seen his fair share of earthquakes.

UNTIL THE NEXT EARTHQUAKE COMES

I had been through two strong earthquakes in a span of twenty years. I know how damaging a quake and its aftershocks can be.

My first frightening experience with such a quake was when I was still a child in Baguio on June 16, 1990. No one was prepared for that 7.2 magnitude earthquake. I had just arrived from elementary school and was just changing into my play clothes when I felt the first strong tremor.

"Run outside, run outside," yelled my father.

I did not know what to do. Our doors slammed shut and it took some effort to open each one. We barely got out when our house collapsed from the strong shaking of the ground.

We were all in shock as the tremors rocked the ground and several buildings around us. I saw how the concrete road near our house crack open, leaving a one meter wide gap. The largest hotel in our city and many other structures collapsed completely, crushing hundreds of hotel employees and guests inside.

I did not know what to make of it because nobody taught us about earthquakes in school. The tremors lasted from late afternoon until early the following morning. Those seemed like the longest hours of our lives.

Many died in the earthquake. Luckily, my entire family survived. However, just like other residents of Baguio City, the experienced traumatized us.

There were massive landslides and the roads to our mountain city were closed. There was no food and water supply. And because we could not go to the areas nearby, we felt trapped in our city. Besides the long brownout that paralyzed practically everything, basic government services were also interrupted. As days wore on, the entire city smelled of garbage and the stench of the dead that remained under the rubble of buildings. It was hard for us to cope with the total destruction that earthquake wrought.

I never imagined that twenty years later, I would again be involved in a similar situation: facing the aftermath of a strong quake. But this time, I was already part of a disaster relief team that offered water-purifying services. Water is always important after any calamity. In Negros Oriental where we were deployed, for example, people had become desperate for drinking water. It had been three days since the quake rocked the area when we arrived. We brought instant noodles, sardines and biscuits, but the people wanted water.

It was hard to set up our water purification system because of the aftershocks. We could barely stand to position our water purification system properly because unlike the people who, by the time we arrived, were already used to the aftershocks, we were still getting used to the constant tremors.

The people lined up for our water despite the dangers of the aftershocks.

"We will die if we do not drink anything now," they said. We assured them that we would have enough for everybody because our system could filter even the muddiest and dirtiest water and make it potable.

We talked to the victims as they lined up for purified water. The trauma was very palpable. It was the same trauma I felt twenty years earlier.

"Why are you crying?" I ask a teenager lining up for water.

"I am the only survivor in my entire family," he meekly replied. Then he retreated into his private world again. He was silent as he waited for his turn to get water.

We stayed for weeks in that earthquake-damaged town and I was thankful for having rendered service to the people even if it was

UNTIL THE NEXT EARTHQUAKE COMES

Earthquakes and landslides cause untold misery to victims.

just water we had to offer. I was thankful that I survived that earthquake twenty years ago and had the proper perspective to face those victims. I was thankful that my family managed the trauma of that disaster well. It could take years before victims grasp the reality of what they had just survived. The psychological damage wrought by a powerful force of nature that can interrupt lives in ways unimaginable can be even worse when one is caught totally unprepared.

I pray that an earthquake like this will not happen again. I know that deep in my heart, however, an earthquake will come as suddenly as the one that disrupted our lives in 1990 and that of the people of Guihulngan, Negros Oriental twenty years later.

George Ayadi

08

LANDSLIDE

LANDSLIDE

A landslide is normally triggered by continuous heavy rainfall or by earthquakes. Other factors that contribute to landslides are high degrees of weathering, fracturing of rocks, deforestation of mountain slopes and the overloading of slope surfaces by structures built on them.

You must always be alert for the possibility of a landslide. Most of these come without warning. A landslide may be slow or rapid, striking with little or no warning. It can be a small landslide or a huge avalanche of river mud or "slurry." But even a small one can become bigger and deadlier as it travels several kilometers, growing in size as the force of the slurry uproots and carries rocks and trees in its path.

You must always be alert for the possibility of a landslide.

BE WARY OF LANDSLIDE-PRONE AREAS

You can avoid being a victim of landslides. The first thing you can do if you are planning to build a house is to check the Mines and Geosciences Bureau (MGB) website to check the landslide susceptibility of your desired location. Consult an experienced professional regarding the most appropriate engineering measures and architectural designs for landslide mitigation or prevention. If you have to build your house in an area that has a slight risk of landslide, make sure that you reinforce the foundation and walls to prevent erosion.

If you are in the countryside, refrain from building your home along a cliff or ridge that has a muddy slope. Be doubly careful if there are no trees to hold the soil together. These are most often prone to landslides.

You can avoid being a landslide victim if you choose your house location well.

This story comes from a rescuer who could not believe how an upscale subdivision on top of a scenic hill could succumb to a landslide triggered by wet and loose soil underneath their houses. It highlights the importance of choosing our house location carefully.

CHERRY HILLS RESCUERS

We were not prepared for a mission like this. Heavy rains poured continuously and we were asked by the mayor of Cainta, Rizal to prepare and position ourselves where we can be of service in case we are needed.

Upon reaching the Cainta municipal hall, we got a report that a building inside a subdivision in neighboring Antipolo had collapsed. I was ordered to bring an ambulance to the site. Two medical aides and I went off on a rescue mission in the middle of the night. We had no idea where the victims were, nor did we know exactly what had happened.

The subdivision was dark and eerily silent. There was a total blackout and for a while, I thought we were sent to the wrong place or perhaps everyone fled. The subdivision must have been so beautiful—houses arranged like terraces were constructed on a hill. At zero visibility, it takes a while to find one's bearings. But as soon as my eyes had become accustomed to the darkness, I realized that a

We never imagined that an entire upscale subdivision on top of a hill would be destroyed by a landslide.

whole section of the terrace-like row of houses had collapsed. And we were the first in.

Without flashlights and just ambulance headlights lighting up the path towards the area that collapsed, we began to see the extent of the damage: houses were piled upon houses, one on top of another. It seemed as if the ground suddenly opened and swallowed hundreds of houses! It was really bad and we knew there were people trapped under the rubble.

We went farther into the subdivision and stopped at the first row of the houses that had collapsed. "Help me! Please!" came a plea from under the rubble. With my flashlight, I searched in the direction of the voice. "I'm here underneath," a woman cried. I realized she was buried somewhere among cement slabs, rubble and wood.

I knew there were more victims trapped under the wreckage of what was once a row of houses. I called in other troops who have already taken their positions in other areas of Cainta.

As we waited for the other troops to arrive, we started digging.

"Help me! please!" came the faint cry again. The troops tried their best to rescue her, but we did not have proper tools—no crowbars or spades. All we had were our knives. One of my soldiers bravely dug into the piles of concrete that were once walls and fences. He knew it posed a big risk even to his own safety, yet he continued with the rescue. He persevered, despite such an enormous challenge. After an hour, a truck from the local electric company brought equipment.

We were able to retrieve her among the piles of cement slabs, cabinets, appliance and furniture. Unfortunately, she succumbed to her injuries on her way to the hospital.

With the first rays of the morning sun came the horrible sight of the devastation. An entire subdivision that sat on a hill collapsed, bringing with it the lives of hundreds of residents of Cherry Hills. That was in 2004.

For a whole month, we continued our retrieval operations, digging up at least 60 bodies. There were many more we could not reach because we did not know where their remains were. Though we were unable to dig those up, I knew that those we found provided closure for their families. That was all we could do.

Sergeant Major Jaime Condino

DETECTING LANDSLIDE SIGNS

There are always telltale signs that a landslide may be in the offing. One of the first indicators is whether trees remain upright on the hill slopes. If you see trees gradually tilt, then this is an indication of soil movement. If you see electric posts or coconut trees slant when they used to stand upright, the area these are planted on

There are always telltale signs of an impending landslide.

may have loosened and therefore prone to landslides.

Another indicator of a landslide coming are cracks on the ground. Long and extended cracks may fill with water and eventually come apart, thereby causing a landslide.

If you live in a community identified as landslide-prone, be alert at all times. Especially when there are intense, short bursts of heavy rains, there are great chances of a landslide.

There will be sounds to indicate that a landslide is dangerously imminent. It will start out as faint, rumbling sounds that increase in volume. As the landslide nears, you will hear trees cracking and boulders being forced down. A trickle of flowing debris may precede a much larger movement of slurry.

INDICATORS IN YOUR HOME

There are signs even in your home signaling the possibility of a landslide. Most of the indicators will come from soil movement under the foundation of your house.

With soil moving, your doors or windows may jam or stick

Be wary when you see abnormal cracks on your walls because your house might be sitting on a landslide-prone slope.

INDICATORS IN YOUR HOME

for the first time. Outside walls, retaining walls or fences may begin pulling away from the main house foundation. Utility poles or trees beside your house may tilt or move. There may also appear slowly developing but widening cracks on the ground, on your driveway or floor. Your water line may break and spew water to the surface. If you spot these indicators and your house is situated on a hill or an elevated portion, it might be in danger of a landslide. Take precautions and consult your engineers.

WHAT TO DO IF CAUGHT IN A LANDSLIDE

Should a landslide catch you, the first thing to do is get out of the path of the downward-flowing slurry. There may be a sturdy building or a big tree that you can climb quickly to get out of the danger zone. Stay up and out of the debris flow.

Do not run down along the path of the flow. Never follow a stream or creek, no matter how convenient and fast, running along it would be. If you find yourself in the mountains, go to the thickly-vegetated slopes, away from the denuded ones. Run across and not flee downwards. The slurry will surely catch you if you do.

Should you survive, be cautious of succeeding landslides. Stay away from the general direction of the landslides until the threat disappears.

Landslides can be prevented if people are responsible about the environment. The Real, Quezon tragedy was caused by illegal logging in the forests around the town. When there were no more trees to hold the water, a giant mass of mud came down burying hundreds of villagers in that coastal town. This next story comes from one of the first rescuers in the Real and Infanta, Quezon tragedy.

A LANDSLIDE FIRST RESPONDER SPEAKS

I was not at all prepared for the situation I found myself in. It was barely a week into military training in October 2004 and as we went about our usual drills and exercises, our trainer suddenly said, "Prepare to go down to Real."

It had been raining continuously in Tanay, Rizal, where our camp was. It had not occurred to us that a calamity had already hit neighboring areas because we had neither radios nor television. Real town in Rizal was less than a hundred kilometers from where we were.

We packed everything we thought could help: utility ropes, food and even our government-issued blankets. We did not know that our rescue mission would take one full month.

Our truck stopped several kilometers from the town because the road was no longer passable. We had to walk the remainder of the distance. The effects of the landslide were already evident around us—and it was still a good two-day hike to get to the town proper. Trees uprooted and felled by rushing mud lay strewn on the roads. The houses we passed seemed deserted. Mud inside these houses was waist deep. We wondered if those who lived in those houses even had the chance to leave.

The food and equipment we carried were heavy, yet we were motivated to move on. After another day and night of walking, we finally reached Real, a coastal town.

Logs of all sizes—those the size of a man's torso to really huge ones, those as big as trucks, were strewn all over. These illegally cut logs were stored on the riverbanks in the mountains. When the heavy rains fell, the trees left were no longer sufficient to hold the water rushing toward Real. Instead, massive volumes of mud took with it the stored logs, wreaking great havoc on the town.

I could not believe what I saw: waist-deep in many areas, chest-deep in some—mud covered everything and made moving so difficult. There were survivors, all of them thirsty because the land-slides contaminated their drinking water. We gave them our rations, enough only for us and just for two days. Luckily, supplies brought

Retrieving the cadavers trapped by mud was a difficult mission for us,
the first responders.

in by ships and aircraft arrived. Relieved but still sad because of the
loved ones they lost, the survivors led us to their homes for us to dig.
The difficult part of our mission was yet to come.

There were bodies neatly laid out in the gymnasium. Their
faces showed how much they tried to fight off mud and water. We
dug out mud in every house we were brought to. And almost always,
we had to recover a body, by then already in decay.

We did that for four weeks. Each time we recovered a body,
we shared the relief and sadness each survivor felt. The death toll
reached thousands, so it is not difficult to imagine how much work
we put in.

It was tiring work, but very fulfilling, especially when we saw
the beginning of what was to become a slow recovery. We left Real
just a few days before Christmas. Our experience there as young soldiers gave us a glimpse of the role we need to play besides fighting
and firing our guns: serving our countrymen during disasters.

Sergeant Eric Gao-ay

Many landslides are avoidable and even preventible. One of the things that you can do to avoid a landslide altogether is to keep away from hazard-prone and risky areas in your community. If you decide to challenge nature, it is just a matter of time when you shall succumb to its forces. There is enough information out there that clearly presents the hazards in your area. Check these out first before you choose a location. You can do this by checking the Mines and Geosciences Bureau website at: www.mgb.org.ph or calling them at (02) 928 8642. The information contained here may save your life.

The Mines and Geosciences Bureau website has valuable information for your safety.

Since landslides are often caused by heavy rainfall and winds, you might also want to check out the PAGASA website at www.pagasa.dost.gov.ph/ or call them at (02) 434 2696.

AVOIDABLE LANDLIDES

The PAGASA website has updated information on incoming typhoons
and possible landslides.

For more information on landslide risks, you can also check
the NDRRMC site at www.ndrrmc.gov.ph/.

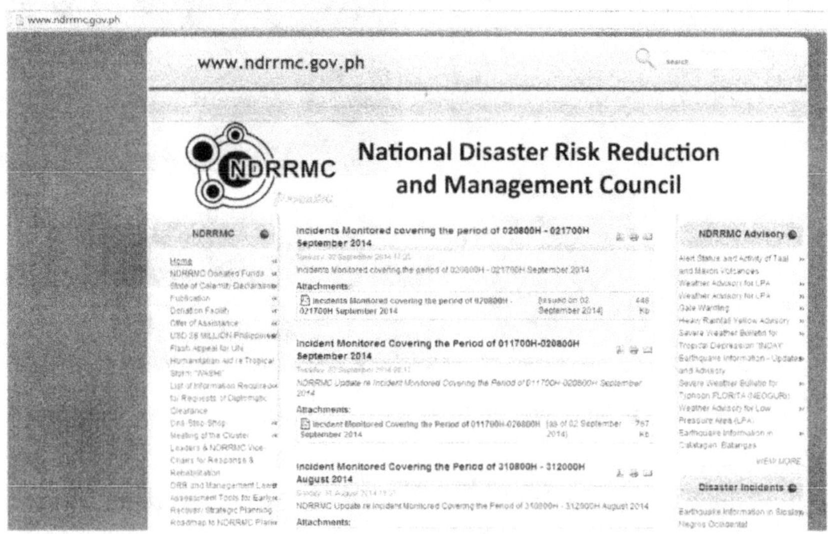

The NDRRMC site offers comprehensive information on disaster
management in major catastrophes like landslides.

09

STORM SURGE

STORM SURGE

The super typhoon Yolanda death toll was aggravated by a series of storm surges that hit the shorelines of affected Leyte and Samar towns in succession. Studies made after it hit the Visayas in 2013 pointed out that the public did not sufficiently understand storm surges. The lay man's disaster vocabulary did not include this.

A strong tropical cyclone has low atmospheric pressure. This creates a shallower coast, creating a potentially high surge. This storm surge causes big waves that can sweep the coastline and extend several kilometers inland. This sudden rise in sea levels will engulf low—lying coastal areas, wreck properties and claim lives.

The lack of public understanding about storm surges caused the most deaths in super typhoon Yolanda in 2013.

A storm surge could sweep hundred meters or even a few kilometers inland. This is the story of a father whose children continue to cope with their trauma after a super typhoon affected their house. Their home was not in a coastal area but was nevertheless affected by the storm surge.

THE TRAUMA OF MY CHILDREN

I know it will take a long time for my children to recover from the trauma of super typhoon Yolanda. Beyond the destruction of property and lives, damage lingers. For some, the tragic memories may last for years, maybe forever. I pray that my children will get over the tragedy of the super typhoon in our place in Tacloban soon.

I was away from home, earning a living in Manila when the typhoon struck. My wife told me that the winds were not as strong at first. In the beginning, I got regular updates from my wife. Then I completely lost contact with her at 6 am. The following day, I was distraught, frustrated and fearful of what may have happened to my family.

I thought about my kids and how they were coping. In the face of a total media blackout due to damaged telecom and broadcast facilities, I did not hear about my place, Tacloban, until 48 hours later. What I saw on TV, the utter and complete destruction of our city by the sea. It was beyond horror. I was lucky to get a ticket home. Upon my arrival, everything looked and smelled disgusting. There was total chaos — relief goods lay disorganized everywhere. Volunteers were confused.

I carried the box of groceries on my back as I walked home. There were no jeepneys nor cabs to hail. Everything in the local Tacloban economy just stopped.

People cautioned me not to proceed because it was getting dark and the complete brownout in the entire city made walking among the debris totally dangerous. But I had to go, no matter what. I had to walk the seven kilometers home just to see my family. I did not know if they were even alive because I had lost contact with them for a few days.

I could barely make my way through the fallen trees, electric posts, and debris as I walked home. It was hard to remember where our house was because all the landmarks were gone. I had no flashlight and all I knew was that I was still following the road that reeked

THE TRAUMA OF MY CHILDREN

of the stench of death as corpses lay just about everywhere. I just prayed that my children did not see this destruction. But it was not so.

The moment I saw my family, I was the happiest man alive! They were all safe and sound. While everything was lost, only one in my family was missing and presumed dead, my father. But my children and my wife were alive.

My eldest child was the first to cry. It was her birthday on that day that I arrived and she was just numb with joy when she saw me.

"Happy birthday!" I greeted her. But she started sobbing as she started to tell the horror of the previous days. She recounted how sea water came in flooding our house. We lived a few kilometers from the sea but they knew it was sea water because it was salty.

"I had to save my sister, Dad!" she cried. Then she told me that her sibling was stuck in the rest room when the water from the storm surge came in.

"Had I not pulled her back, she would have drowned," she tearfully narrated. Between her sobbing and her stories, I knew that it would take time before she fully recovered.

Then it was my second child's turn to tell his story. Among my three children, he was the most reserved. On the second day, when I was not yet around, one of my relatives came to fetch my son so they could walk the seven kilometers to the airport. At that time, relief goods were in the airport. Victims had to go there to pick up relief goods.

"There were many dead people in the streets, Dad!" he started his story.

"There were children like me, dead in the streets," he continued. Then he began to sob and was on the verge of breaking down.

"There were many mothers looking for their kids," he continued. I did not know what to say, but I knew that my only son was just letting it all out. He obviously had such a harrowing experience that he no longer wanted to venture out of the house.

My kids were most affected by the storm surge and typhoon.

"I will get you out of our city, son," I assured him. I knew it was going to be hard to start over in a new place but my family had so many tragic memories that their continued stay in Tacloban could never erase.

We relocated to Batangas, where there are lesser risks—or so we thought. Less than a year after super typhoon Yolanda, another powerful storm crossed Laguna and Batangas. This time I was with my family. It was so painful for me to see the trauma that scarred my youngest child, only five years old.

"I am here, my daughter," I told her when the rains and the thunderstorms began. I saw her seek shelter under the dining table, afraid and shocked. I went down and asked her to come out of her hiding place.

"You are safe now with Dad," I told her. Yet there was something about the rains and the thunderstorms that disturbed her.

THE TRAUMA OF MY CHILDREN

It pained me to realize that my children continued to harbor traumas because of the super typhoon. I pray silently that the shock, the fear, the insecurity inside their young hearts and minds will go away soon.

Avelino Velasco

PRIVATE SECTOR DISASTER RESPONSE

The Philippine private sector has a very important role to play in disaster preparedness, relief, recovery and reconstruction. Corporations and their corporate social responsibility arms can focus on early recovery efforts for shelter, livelihood, sanitation, health and infrastructure.

One of the main organizations set up by the private sector to put up a more organized disaster response is the Philippine Disaster Recovery Foundation. The creation of this entity was spearheaded by the Philippine Long Distance Telephone Co. (PLDT), Ayala Corporation, Aboitiz Equity Ventures, Philippine Chamber of Commerce and Industry (PCCI), Makati Business Club (MBC), Management Association of the Philippines (MAP), Bankers Association of the Philippines (BAP) and other NGO's. This entity seeks to be a major point of contact of the private sector with the government and international aid agencies and organizations.

With the aggressiveness of the private sector to help out, Philippine communities stand to benefit significantly. However, it would take the Filipino nation working together -- local government leaders, public servants in government agencies, the all-too important private sector, volunteers from local and international NGOs, community volunteers and citizens -- to truly make our communities disaster-resilient.

VOLCANIC ERUPTION

VOLCANIC ERUPTION

Though not as frequent and regular as typhoons, volcanic eruptions are extremely destructive. One eruption could bury an entire town and destroy a large area. The lahars could bury communities and render agricultural lands useless for decades.

There are 22 active volcanoes in the Philippines. The six most active ones are Mayon in Albay, Taal in Batangas, Bulusan in Sorsogon, Kanlaon in Negros Oriental, Hibok-Hibok in Camiguin and Pinatubo, which straddles Zambales, Pampanga and Tarlac.

Taal has erupted 47 times, the last of which was on October 3, 1977. Mayon volcano is closely monitored by the Philippine Institute of Volcanology and Seismology (PHIVOLCS) as it has registered 49 eruptions. The Kanlaon volcano has recorded 21 eruptions, the latest of which was August 1996. Long thought to be dormant, Pinatubo suddenly erupted in June 1991 covering most of Luzon in ash and burying entire towns in lahar. Bulusan's last eruption was on November 27, 1994, its 18th. Hibok-Hibok in Camiguin is a complex volcano, having erupted only 5 times. However, the last of these eruptions began in September 1948 and lasted until July 1953.

The eruption of Pinatubo caught everyone by surprise. The volcano spewed ash as high as 30 kilometers in the air, covering up to 500 kilometers across. I remember not being able to come home to the Philippines after my first two years at West Point, largely because flights were cancelled that time.

So massive was the economic effect of this eruption even on surrounding areas that it was felt for years. Flowing lahar not only destroyed crops and crop cycles, it also induced flooding. Such is the power of volcanic eruptions.

A blind man I know survived the eruption of Mount Pinatubo in 1991. While his family did not lose any members, his entire community lost everything when lahar from the erupting volcano buried their village.

I am now blind. My left eye was permanently damaged when a holdupper assaulted us at a bus terminal about twenty years ago. We were desperate for jobs after lahar from Mount Pinatubo buried our town of Bacolor in Pampanga. Without any source of livelihood, most of us ventured outside our province and even abroad for work.

Our village about 45 kilometers from Mount Pinatubo was totally destroyed and buried in lahar.

I will never forget that day on June 15, 1990, when Mount Pinatubo, a long dormant volcano about 45 kilometers away from our town, erupted in full fury.

Most of us did not know that a volcano was nearby. It had long been inactive so residents like me regarded it more as a huge mountain.

"It is the end of the world!" a neighbor shouted. We rushed outside to see what was happening. Then we saw what a volcanic eruption was really like.

WHEN PINATUBO ERUPTED

Everything grew dark, so dark that we could not see anymore. I had never experienced complete darkness like that. It must have been so because the ashes spewing from the volcano had so totally obstructed the sun. Then the tremors started. Every time the earth moved, a hail of ashes and small rocks would come falling.

"I got hit by a rock!" shouted a neighbor. Before I could run for cover, a fist-size, hot rock also hit me. It hurt because the hot rocks came directly from the volcano. We all went inside our homes to seek shelter from the continuous hail of rocks and ashes.

I will never forget the frantic cries of those around me. it seemed like our entire village was hysterical. "It is the end of the world!" people kept saying. We were afraid the volcano would make a final eruption and bury us all.

Amid the regular aftershocks and the endless ash fall, nobody slept well, if at all. The following morning the aftershocks had decreased in frequency. The ashes had slowed down. As we surveyed our still hazy surroundings, we saw that our entire village looked like a winter wonderland, except that it was not snow that blanketed our surroundings, but fresh, gray ash from the volcano's belly.

"Many people died!" was the first news the village crier brought. In areas near the volcano, there were reports that many were overcome by flowing lava. Others reported that the initial flow of hot molten materials and lahar had severely damaged houses along the rivers.

We never imagined that an eruption almost fifty kilometers away would affect our community until after 5 years later.

Nobody in our town had ever heard of lahar until that time. But we would later experience this grayish, sandy soil that came down the slopes of the volcano every time it rained. Thus, we found out that there was enough lahar deposited along the sides and the crater of the volcano that could carpet the surrounding towns like ours with at least 30 feet of lahar.

WHEN PINATUBO ERUPTED

The first time it rained, we immediately moved out without taking anything with us. As we rushed to the evacuation center, we saw the lahar flow, gradually enveloping up our village. It took a few days before we were able to go back.

The next time it rained, we did the same thing. But when we headed back to our homes after a short stay at the evacuation center, we found that more lahar had accumulated, so much more than we could put away.

Two years passed and we had slowly begun to accept that lahar will soon engulf our entire town. And true enough, the volcanologists were proven right as lahar did flow continuously for four years. By that time, all our houses were submerged in lahar. There were no indications at all that houses once stood there because lahar had totally buried our homes.

We were not alone. There were many more towns and villages along the lahar's path that suffered the same fate.

All of us lost everything—our homes, livelihood-- everything. In the face of such a grim scenario, most of us had to leave our town to seek opportunities elsewhere.

It had been twenty three years since Pinatubo erupted. I am now completely blind, making a living as a masseur. The memories are still vivid in my mind. The total darkness we experienced was a preview of my life now—I remember how those vain attempts to see in the dark felt then, as I know now how vain my efforts to see the light once more would be.

Sonny Bautista

DISASTER-RESILIENT COMMUNITIES

The hazards of nature are beyond our control, yet there are measures that we can do to minimize the severe impact of a volcanic eruption, or any disaster for that matter.

DISASTER-RESILIENT COMMUNITIES

With proactive disaster risk reduction and management systems in place, damage to properties and unnecessary casualties can be avoided.

One of the things you can do is check out the website of the PHIVOLCS at http://www.phivolcs.dost.gov.ph for information related to volcanic eruptions and earthquakes. The valuable information in this site might be useful to save your life.

The PHIVOLCS site has the most extensive information about volcanic eruptions and earthquakes.

You might also want to visit the risk maps at www.geoportal.gov.ph. The information here may help you decide how to ensure the safety of your family.

The Philippine Geoportal site has the most complete collection of risk maps.

Mayon Volcano has erupted quite a number of times that cities and towns surrounding its base circumference of 62.6 kilometers say that there are telltale signs of an impending eruption.

The people around Mayon Volcano have natural ways of predicting imminent eruption. When creeks and rivers run dry for several continuous months, they know that Mayon will erupt soon.

Always with a visible flow of lava, especially menacing on dark nights when you can see the flaming red hot lava on top, Mayon is always dangerously threatening. When the residents hear rumblings, roars and sense earthquakes, and the lava on the crater becomes more active, an eruption is about to occur.

When wild boars and chickens scurry away from the volcano that means that the volcano is about to erupt.

If you reside near an active volcano or are a visitor to the volcano, watch on TV, listen to the radio or get internet advisories on possible eruption. If a warning is issued, you must leave immediately.

When you sense early warning signs of an eruption, flee the area in haste.

BEFORE THE ERUPTION

Unlike other catastrophes, there are often clear signs of an impending volcanic eruption. Thus, you must take advantage of the time before the eruption to take all precautionary measures and move your family to safety. There is no time to waste prior to an eruption.

You must leave the area immediately. Many of the fatalities in recent eruptions were those who refused to heed the warnings.

Should you need to travel down a volcano to evacuate, do not cross geothermal areas. Geysers, mud spots and hotspots are common volcanic area features. The ground around these are thin and you could fall into one of these.

There are many dangers associated with a volcanic eruption. The first is pyroclastic flow that could burn or kill you. These are hot rocks or debris sent flying by the erupting volcano. Get away from their range. Or if you cannot, go to nearby hills or ridgeline that would protect you from these.

Get to high ground at all cost. Lahar, deadly lava flows and mudflows — effects of a volcanic eruption, travel to low-lying areas, dry creeks and streams. Stay off these valleys and river beds until the danger is over.

Go away, as far as you can from the volcano. Pyroclastic flow can travel over 500 kilometers. Until you are truly out of the range of these deadly pyroclastics, you are not out of danger from the volcanic eruption.

Stay inside if you live in a strong, elevated structure. Close the windows and remove anything outside that easily catches fire. A red-hot pyroclastic flow— or hot clouds of ash and gas - can ignite a roof or any combustible material very quickly.

If you are indoors, look out for fires and watch out for collapsing roofs. Many of the victims of the Pinatubo eruption died in their homes when their roofs collapsed from the weight of the accumulated ash.

You must know the safety measures during a volcanic eruption. If you have to scamper to safety at the last minute, do not cross a lava flow or lahar. You run the risk of being trapped between flows if another lava flow is coming. Besides, you might step into a thin crust of lava that looks cool, yet it is just a thin layer over a core of extremely hot lava.

Protect yourself from the deadly gases. The eruption emits hazardous gases that affect people especially with asthma or respiratory problems. Wear a gas mask or if none is available, use a moist piece of cloth. This will temporarily protect your lungs from inhaling the deadly fumes. Do not stay low on the ground because the deadliest gases accumulate near the ground.

Protect your eyes. If you have swim goggles have the children wear these. Their sensitive eyes will be protected from the dust and ash.

Be prepared against the deadly fumes from the erupting volcano.

AFTER THE ERUPTION

Pick up the pieces after an eruption. Scrape off the accumulated ash on your roof to prevent its collapse. Clean the roof and gutter with water to prevent clogging.

Shake ash loose from all furniture and curtains. Wash them first before you hang your draperies again. Do not use a bar of soap because rubbing one against cloth only embeds the ash deeper into the fabric. Use powdered detergent instead.

Do not assume that your traditional water source is still safe. It might have been contaminated by the lava and gases. Thoroughly wash all fruits and vegetables before cooking these.

Expect lahar to accumulate on your roofs after an eruption. Clean these up with care.

TSUNAMI

TSUNAMIS

There have been several local tsunami incidents in the past. In 1976, one hit the Southwest Coast of Mindanao after a 7.9 magnitude earthquake hit the Moro Gulf. More than 3,000 were left dead and 12,000 families rendered homeless. There were also other tsunami cases in various parts of the archipelago during the past decades.

The coastal areas facing the South China Sea and Pacific Ocean are at risk from locally-generated tsunamis. Since the Philippines is prone to earthquakes, every time the ground trembles, there is a possibility of a tsunami. In the case of a locally-generated tsunami, there will not be enough time to warn people. The first big wave is often followed by a succeeding gigantic wave, 2 to 5 minutes after the first one.

Earthquakes in countries bordering the Pacific Ocean like Alaska, Chile or Japan can cause tsunamis, which can also affect our country. The travel times for the big waves may be from one to 24 hours, which should give coastal communities time to evacuate.

A tsunami from thousands of kilometers away can hit your community without warning.

TSUNAMI EVACUATION

You do not have the luxury of long preparation time prior to the arrival of a tsunami. When an alert is called, leave immediately.

Leave your things. There is no time to delay. Your life is more important than your belongings.

Move away from the coast into high ground, even into hills and mountains. If you do not have time to move out, climb the highest and sturdiest building nearest you. Do not go inside buildings made of light materials as these could collapse. Go up the roof of the tallest building and stay there until the water recedes.

Should you not have any other option, climb a large tree. Do not go for smaller ones that could break and snap under the force of the water.

Assist your kids and the elderly members of your family. Teach your children in advance how to float and survive. The strength of the tsunami waves might bring you to different directions.

Stay together as a family. Make sure that you have set a pre determined point where you will gather later just in case you get separated.

In an impending tsunami, go to the highest and toughest building in your area.

SIGNS OF A TSUNAMI

An earthquake often precedes a tsunami. When you are in a coastal area, and you feel the ground shaking, be warned of a possible

SIGNS OF A TSUNAMI

tsunami. The big waves could come in a matter of minutes or a few hours.

Be alert for rapid rise and fall of coastal waters. When the sea suddenly recedes, leaving bare sand and coral, this is a major warning sign of a tsunami or a storm surge. When the sea retreats, you will see stranded fish and sea life. Do not flock to the shoreline. Run away inland as fast as you can. You will have 2 minutes at best before the tsunami arrives.

When the water recedes, run away fast because a tsunami is incoming.

IF YOU GET CAUGHT BY TSUNAMI WATERS

Remember that tsunamis are a series of waves. One can be separated from the other tsunami wave in very short or very long periods of time. Just because the first one was not as huge and deadly does not mean you can bring your alertness level down. The next tsunami wave might be huge and deadly.

Should tsunami waves catch you, it is time to practice all the survival swimming skills you know.

Go with the current. Never fight it. Grab anything that floats — an empty water container, a bamboo pole, log or banana trunk. Go with the current until you find the opportunity to paddle to land and get out of the water.

Avoid debris. Second only to drowning, being struck by debris is the second major cause of death during tsunamis.

If you are out in the sea when the tsunami strikes, do not go ashore. Instead, take your boat in the opposite direction and head farther out to sea. While the danger of big tsunami waves is also in the middle of the sea, there are not as many debris. Remember that debris such as logs, steel bars and sharp objects are as deadly as the tsunami waves.

Be alert and keep cool and you will survive the tsunami.

Tsunamis are a series of big, dangerous waves.

AFTER THE TSUNAMI

Expect massive devastation in the aftermath of a tsunami. There will be debris all over, destroyed infrastructure, dead bodies around. Fresh water will be out and food supplies will be disrupted.

Do not go down from your evacuation or refugee area until all the water has subsided and you are sure that there are no more follow-on tsunami waves.

Keep hydrated with coconut water. Do not grab food strewn around because these had been contaminated by the water.

For food, head inland and look for vegetables and fruits unaffected by the tsunami waves.

Expect massive destruction after a tsunami.

TORNADO

TORNADO

Tornadoes can strike any time of the day – but these develop more often in the afternoons. When the temperature is highest, tornadoes may also develop in the evening, though less frequently.

Moving erratically, a tornado is a violently rotating column of air that ravage trees, structures and even animals along its path. The trademark outline of a tornado is a funnel-like column of black air, the narrow end of which touches the ground just like a vacuum cleaner.

Signs of a tornado forming include a funnel- shaped column at the base of a cumulonimbus cloud. The weather will be warm and humid but deceptively calm. Normally, you will see lightning flashes and hear thunder. When the tornado touches the ground, there will be a roaring and buzzing sound.

Often obscured by rain or dust, it always leaves a path of destruction. Lasting just a few minutes, the 45 km per hour winds destroy and bring to its vortex things in its path.

A funnel-shaped column of dark swirling cloud indicates an incoming tornado.

TORNADOES AND THUNDERSTORMS

A thunderstorm may occur when there are distant rumbling sounds, flashes of lightning, towering cumulonimbus clouds and quickly darkening skies. When a thunderstorm develops, it is a violent atmospheric disturbance accompanied by thunder, rain, lightning and strong gusts of wind. Normally, a thunderstorm will last about 30 minutes and will affect a local area 5 kilometers in diameter.

There are hazards associated with thunderstorms, the most dangerous of which is lightning. With the temperature of the lightning volt five times hotter than the surface of the sun, this is very dangerous to anyone struck by it.

Thunderstorms and tornadoes develop together.

A thunderstorm can also trigger a tornado or a water spout. If this happens, expect destructive effects of a thunderstorm.

Tornadoes and thunderstorms go together. Tornadoes usually only develop with thunderstorms, though the thunderstorm might

TORNADOES AND THUNDERSTORMS

be far from where you are. Thus, it is important to be alert for a tornado when there are thunderstorms and there is a strong, continuous rotation of the cloud base. During or right after a thunderstorm, it is unusually calm and quiet. Then a faint roar is heard. When you hear a sound of a train or jet rumble and skies darken, it is likely that a tornado is approaching. If you still have time, secure outdoor objects first like garden tools, signs, garden sets and garbage cans. These can become deadly flying missiles during the tornado's passage.

Go inside and find the most interior room either on the first floor or if you have one, a basement. Do not stand by windows or bookshelves that can possibly fall on you.

Keep calm and you should weather the tornado.

WHEN A TORNADO STRIKES

It is extremely dangerous to be out in an open field when a tornado strikes. Lie down, stay close to the ground and cover your

When a tornado approaches, lie down and duck to the ground.

head. Find a depression on the ground. If possible a shelter is better than being exposed to open terrain. Do not attempt to outrun a tornado.

If you are driving a car, stop and abandon it. Seek shelter at the nearest ditch, ravine, culvert or natural depression. Try to avoid hiding under a bridge or overpass.

WATER SPOUT

Tornadoes are not a common phenomenon in the Philippines. Locally known as *"buhawi,"* these destructive but brief natural occurrences happen without warning.

More frequent than land — based tornadoes are the water spouts. When a tornado forms and moves above a body of water, it develops into a water spout. Though less violent and deadly than the land-based tornado, a water spout can cause flooding in areas where it deposits the water that it gathers in its funnel.

There were instances when a waterspout moved inland, wreaking destruction in coastal towns. In Gingoog City in Northern Mindanao, 1,000 families were rendered homeless in 1979 when a water spout came ashore.

One of the soldiers tasked to run a rescue mission to save people in the tornado aftermath in Digos City in 2013 had not seen a tornado before. The only report he got was that the people in the ricefields in the outskirts of the city saw a giant, swirling mass of the dark clouds in the vicinity, the tornado sucked all the objects including water in its path. Then it would dump the water when the clouds could no longer take the weight. Water that flowed to the river flooded parts of Digos City - all without rain.

People in this part of the Southern Mindanao have reported infrequent but almost annual sightings of a tornado. The effects of the previous ones were confined to smaller uninhabited areas. All they saw were the signature black, debris — laden swirling winds and clouds of the tornado.

WATER SPOUT

This one was different because it struck fear in the hearts of the people along the river banks and seashores. Most of them could not believe that flashfloods will affect their villages without rain. It never happened to them before.

They were just so relieved to see the rescuers bring their ropes and gear to bring them out.

A water spout is very dangerous to people living in coastal areas.

LIGHTNING STORMS

Lightning strikes claim lives annually. Therefore, you should exercise caution when there is a lightning storm.

If you are in the countryside, avoid building your house in the middle of rice fields or barren hills. The structure you build is all the lightning needs. In an open field, lightning tends to strike whatever is highest or tallest.

If you are outdoor and you are out in the mountains during a lightning storm, find a cave or crevice of a large tree to hide in. Big logs or rocks are also good shelters against lightning. Avoid being near places like rivers or creeks during lightning strikes. These often attract lightning.

Should you be near your home, head inside immediately. Close the door and windows and turn off all appliances to avoid attracting lightning to your home.

The rule of thumb during lightning storms is to avoid anything made of metal or electrical. Do not use a landline phone in a lightning storm. Lightning can travel to the home through landlines. Avoid power lines as these are conductors of electricity. Do not lean against anything made of metal, because if the lightning strikes it, you will surely feel the heat generated by the lightning. Get out of the swimming pool and bath tubs. The water conducts electricity and so do the swimming pool railings.

If you find yourself inside a car, do not lean against its metal sides. Do not use the car radio and make sure all windows are closed.

During a lightning storm, avoid getting near anything that conducts electricity.

LIGHTNING STORMS

When a lightning strikes, move out of soccer fields, parade grounds or golf courses. When you are taller than everything else around you, just as when you are in a field, chances of getting struck by the lightning increases.

If you are travelling with a group, position yourselves 15 to 30 meters apart. This will reduce the risk of lightning traveling through each person.

If you are wearing a backpack with a metal frame, remove it from your body. Stay at least 50 meters away from your backpack.

If your are wearing portable electronics, especially headphones which have cable electronics, remove them immediately. This will lessen the likelihood of a severe injury to your ears in case a lightning strikes.

If you have time, wear a pair of rubber shoes or boots. Rubber does not conduct electricity and your rubber shoes might just save your life.

Wear rubber shoes and put distance between yourselves during a lightning strike.

13

FIRE

FIRE

Among the human-induced disasters, fire is one of the most destructive. When fire hits your home, chances of recovering your possessions are slim. When fire engulfs your neighborhood, there is incalculable danger to your life and property. Thus, it is very important for you to be prepared in case of fire. Fires are avoidable unless a fire is triggered by arson. Many of the fires that happen are caused entirely by human fault or negligence.

While we must be alert at preventing fires, we must prepare all measures to control smoke in case of fire. The leading cause of death during a fire, by a three-to-one ratio over burns, is asphyxiation. When one inhales the smoke from fire, choking occurs. This causes death.

One of the worst tragedies that hit my wife's family was when her brother, sister-in-law and niece died with several others in a hotel fire. The bodies were recovered huddled in an embrace on their hotel room floor. Obviously, they died of asphyxiation.

A damaging fire can destroy your home and all your precious belongings.

One of the most common causes of fire is faulty electrical wiring. In an effort to save money, some families resort to hiring the services of unlicensed electricians. These people do not have the required skills and often recommend the use of unsafe electrical wiring. Hire a licensed electrician and buy safe wiring for your home.

Do not smoke in bed. Crush cigarette butts thoroughly before discarding these. Do not throw cigarette butts into waste baskets. Before emptying your ashtray, make sure the contents are cold.

Remove fire hazards by keeping everything clean. Dispose off paper and garbage especially where members of your family usually relax to smoke. Always have an ash tray available in areas at home for smoking visitors.

Do not overload electrical outlets with several appliances. Consider plugging only one high-voltage appliance into a socket. Do not place combustible materials near bulbs.

Never place candles and lamps beside curtains. The wind or pets could topple them, causing the curtains to catch fire.

Do not store flammable materials like gasoline in areas that smoking visitors frequent. These will catch fire easily when one careless bystander or visitor throws a cigarette butt on them.

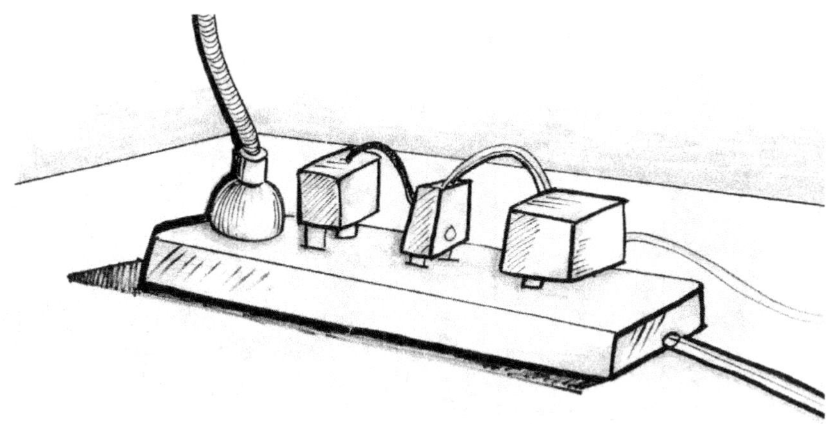

Never clog electrical sockets with several appliances.

PREVENTING FIRE IN THE KITCHEN

The kitchen is where most fires start at home. You must strictly observe fire preventive measures in the kitchen.

Regularly check kerosene and gas stoves for leaks. Invest in a quality LPG tank. The LPG tank that you use can explode and start a fire if you do not turn it off after use. Gases that leak may explode. Make sure that the hose connecting the LPG tank and oven is good and safe. Fix the gas hose stopper firmly so that there are no leaks. Replace an old LPG hose, especially a fragile one, with a new one.

Do not keep flammable materials near the LPG tank. Neither should you place pieces of paper or anything that easily catches fire beside the oven.

Extinguish all live charcoals and embers after cooking. Inspect the kitchen for live fires before retiring for the night.

When you cook, make sure you do not leave for the bedroom or the living room with the stove on. An accident might just trigger a fire as you relax.

Never leave matches and lighters within reach of children. They do not know the damage they can cause by playing with these. Be safe in the kitchen to prevent fire in your home.

Always inspect your LPG tank of leaks.

Do your best to avoid triggering a bushfire. This is deadly and difficult to contain. Do not build a bonfire when it is windy. An ember could fly off to a bunch of dried leaves and set off a forest fire. If you absolutely have to build a bonfire, make sure you have buckets of water filled and within easy reach.

Do not burn your garbage without closely supervising their complete incineration. Do not assume that a heap of garbage had been completely incinerated if the top portion is completely burnt. Check underneath the heap because there might be remaining pieces of garbage that are still being burned. To be sure, dose the burnt heap of garbage with water when you are done burning it. Never burn plastic products or rubber because these have chemical properties that induce fire.

Avoid making torches or lamps that rely on gasoline. The wind or a drunken partygoer, could topple the lamp and start a fire.

Be careful when building bonfires as these may cause fire.

INSURING YOUR POSSESSIONS

There are several insurance companies that offer products to protect your assets from "acts of God" circumstances. They are aggregated in an organization called Philippine Insurers and Reinsurers Association (PIRA). One reputable insurance firm that specializes in protecting you from perils such as fires, earthquakes, typhoons, floods or volcanic eruptions is Standard Insurance (+632 2845-1111, www1.standard-insurance.com). Its Biz Protect product insures businesses such as groceries, supermarkets, salons, restaurants, gas stations and internet shops from these disasters. For its House Protect plan, the respected firm insures your dream house against fire, lightning, and other calamities. For your car, it also has a product that covers your prized vehicle against "acts of nature."

Shop around for the most affordable insurance plan for your possessions. With the regular occurence of floods and other calamities, insuring your assets is one of the best decisions you can make.

One of the most dangerous jobs in the world is to be a firefighter. The following personal narrative comes from a veteran firefighter who has had extensive experience putting out fires in burning buildings, houses, warehouses and slum areas.

A FIREFIGHTER'S LIFE

To be a firefighter is to have one of the most dangerous jobs in the world. I have been a firefighter for several years, and having responded to a number of fires around Metro Manila, I have come up close and personal with death several times.

The riskiest situations happen when we have to break into windows and doors and right into a burning building. We try to avoid this dangerous situation because inside a burning house, it is almost like hell to be inside. Besides the fire and the smoke, you have to watch out for falling wooden beams, chandeliers, and other burning objects. I have had close brushes with death several times as one burning object nearly fell on me as I was inside a burning house.

I have also encountered situations where we have to put out a fire in one of Manila's slum communities. It is often hard to penetrate these areas with our hoses because of the narrow alleys. During these times when we could not bring our fire truck right next to the burning houses, we walk on the rickety roofs of the shacks just to get to the fire. The real danger is when we step on the roofs that may collapse. I dread the possibility of being trapped in a burning shanty made of cheap and readily combustible materials. Yet as a firefighter, I have to face every fire situation as if it were completely unique.

It is never time to be complacent when there is fire. One

It is a very difficult job to be a firefighter.

that I will never forget is when we responded to a fire in a building that had explosives inside. We never encountered such situation before. All of us were shocked when a loud explosion occurred as we were about to enter the burning building. We felt blessed that we were not yet inside when the explosion happened.

We had been to several dangerous fire suppressions since. Each time we do, I pray to God to keep us safe. Every time, we get out alive, we rest and remain alert until the next alarm sounds! After all, that's how things are. I will continue to keep my commitment to this dangerous job for the sake of those we serve.

Eduardo Rapada

DURING A FIRE

Presence of mind can help save lives during a fire. Sound the fire alarm first. Your action will trigger the water sprinkler systems indoors. You may just stop the fire.

If you discover the fire, report it to the fire department immediately. Notify your family and neighbors about the fire, too.

Use a fire extinguisher. A fire can be contained within the first 3 minutes by using a fire extinguisher.

Attempt to compartmentalize the fire. Close the door of the room where the fire originated. This may prevent the fire from spreading. Close the doors behind you as you escape. Before opening a closed door, use the back of your hand to feel it. Do not open it if it is warm because there is fire on the other side.

As you escape, do not use the elevator. Use the stairwells when going down. Leave the building via a fire escape or evacuation equipment, usually installed in the balcony. Never jump out if you still have other exit options. If you are in immediate danger, and your room is not too high, jump. Throw cushions or mattresses first to break your fall.

If the smoke is too thick, crawl. Get a piece of cloth, wet it

If your clothes catch fire, drop and roll over and over until it is extinguished.

and use this to cover your nose and mouth. It is easier to breathe when you are down on the floor because smoke rises.

FIRE IN A BUILDING

Fire in a multi-storey building is hazardous. If you get caught in this situation, make sure that you know fire exits well. Plan your escape around these fire exits. Do not get confused and remember all the exits. Escaping from a fire is a lot easier if you plan your escape in advance. Even in limited visibility, you will know how to react and move out.

Frequent fire drills help office workers stay calm in case a fire breaks out. Make sure to go over the escape plan with your office-mates. The more coordinated and prepared you are, the more lives will be saved. Plan two ways out of every room. Make sure you can unlock all door and window locks, and escape through these quickly, even in the dark.

Always remember that smoke is more dangerous than flames. If you do not think you can extinguish the flames, evacuate fast.

Once you get out, stay out. Do not attempt to go back into a fire because this is extremely risky.

EPILOGUE

Sixty five days ago, as the powerful typhoon Glenda ravaged Metro Manila, Batangas and Laguna, I started writing this book. Today, as I write this epilogue, disasters have struck the Philippines again. As I write this day of 19 September 2014, Mayon Volcano is poised to erupt anytime. Thousands of families have already been evacuated from the 6 to 8 kilometer danger radius. Cebu City has declared a state of calamity because of floods and landslides. There was a 5.1 magnitude earthquake in the southern Mindanao city of General Santos. The heavy rains in Metro Manila overnight had flooded almost the entirety of the metropolis. My family is poised to evacuate to safer places again, just like what we have done for a number of times.

These calamities that come so frequently and regularly will not cease. In fact, another typhoon is poised to strike within a few days as the current one is about to exit. With global warming, overpopulation and abuse of our environment, these could get worse.

I hope that by having read this book, you shall have prepared yourself and your family members for the onslaught of future disasters.

ACKNOWLEDGEMENTS

I thank the people that made this book possible. The victims and first responders who shared their personal stories deserve my most profuse thanks.

I sincerely recognize my team composed of Leoncio Damasin, Tony Relao, Erwin Agustin, Zaldy Liban, Bryan Cañedo, Romy Alpuerto, Nelson Vergara, Adrian Huertas, Cesar Cuenca, Max Lamano, Russell Rodriguez-Galgo, and Analyn Aurelio for their efforts to make this book happen.

I wish to thank the First Scout Ranger Regiment commander, Brigadier General Eduardo Davalan, for his support.

I deeply appreciate Mr. Oscar Advento for doing the artwork for this book.

I also thank my book graphic artist Herwin Barbado for his patience in doing this book.

Many thanks to Ms. Tin Bartolome for editing this book. Thank you also to my young editors, my 11 year old son Rafi and 9 year old daughter Jami.

Most of all, I thank my family - wife Jing, mother Nelia, daughters Deji and Jamina and son Rafi.

ABOUT THE AUTHOR

Lieutenant Colonel Dennis V. Eclarin directly participated in numerous emergency responses to mobilize first responders, deliver relief goods and implement post disaster rehabilitation projects. As the former Chief of the AFP Peace and Development Center, he facilitated partnerships with civic organizations focusing on humanitarian assistance in the aftermath of disasters. The author is a West Point graduate who did extensive combat duty with the elite Philippine Army Scout Rangers where he earned six Gold Cross Medals, the country's third highest military award.

Lieutenant Colonel Eclarin is the first member of the armed services recognized as an Asia Society Asia 21 Young Leader Fellow. He is the only Armed Forces officer conferred the Young Global Leader Award by the World Economic Forum.

www.ingramcontent.com/pod-product-compliance
Lightning Source LLC
Chambersburg PA
CBHW070834250726
48662CB00003B/1229